A Story Behind Every Stone

The Confederate Section
of Oakwood Cemetery
Raleigh, North Carolina

Compiled by Charles E. Purser
Garner, NC
Edited by Frank B. Powell, III
Wake Forest, NC

A Story Behind Every Stone
The Confederate Section of Oakwood Cemetery
Raleigh, North Carolina

Compiled by Charles E. Purser, Jr.
Edited by Frank B. Powell, III
Cover photo by John Gregory

©2005, 2010 The Scuppernong Press

Second Printing

The Scuppernong Press
PO Box 1724
Wake Forest, NC 27588
www.scuppernongpress.com

Library of Congress Control Number: 2010929184

International Standard Book Number (ISBN) 978-0-9845529-1-7

Table of Contents

Editor's Note... iii

Introduction.. vii

Illustrations.. ix

Chapter 1   The Work Behind the Oakwood
            Confederate Cemetery 1

Chapter 2   The Confederate Hospitals
            of Raleigh and Wake County... 7

Chapter 3   Disinterring and Reinterring the Bodies of Our Dead
            by The Ladies Memorial Association of Raleigh, NC..... 11

Chapter 4   The Confederate Cemetery, Raleigh, NC....................... 15

Chapter 5   The Gettysburg Dead in Oakwood............................... 19

Chapter 6   The Arlington Dead in Oakwood................................. 23

Chapter 7   Soldiers' Home... 27

Chapter 8   The Research 31

Chapter 9   Oakwood Confederate Cemetery
            Restoration Committee.. 35

Chapter 10 A Sampling of Stories Behind the Stones...................... 39

Location Map 48-51

Abbreviations and Explanation 52-53

The Alpha Roster of Confederate Soldiers in Oakwood.................... 54

Oakwood Veterans by North Carolina Counties 118

Oakwood Veterans by Rank and States.. 120

Occupations of Oakwood Veterans.. 122

A Story Behind Every Stone

Editor's Note

When I first visited Oakwood Cemetery in Raleigh, the grass was knee high in the Gettysburg section and some of the plain stone markers had sunk deep into the ground. It was obvious the cemetery had been neglected for many years.

During the first efforts to clean the place up, the Oakwood restoration project was born with the thought that every man buried there deserved a proper headstone with his name and personal information inscribed on it. That part of the project is now complete, but the work continues.

Of course, we would not have an Oakwood cemetery without the efforts of the Ladies' Memorial Association which formed in the late 1860s. Considering how destitute the South was dur-

Inside the House of Memory looking at the Gettysburg section.

ing the aftermath of the war in the 1860s and 1870s, I find their accomplishments astonishing. They were very dedicated and kept excellent records. These records, now housed at the North Carolina Archives and History, enabled us to glean most of the information contained within these pages. The old photographs are also from these records. If it was not for these ladies who gave so generously of their time and talent, many of our ancestors would still lie in unmarked graves in lands foreign to them.

Later, members of the United Daughters of the Confederacy became the guardians of Oakwood in the early 1900s and continued the work started by their mothers and grandmothers. They also maintained excellent records which gave us further insight into the lives of the men who lie buried in this hallowed ground.

In the late 1980s, the Sons of Confederate Veterans began the restoration project; most of the modern photographs were taken by various members — too many to mention by name for fear of leaving someone out — but they too deserve our heartfelt thanks and appreciation.

There have been hundreds of volunteers over the years who have worked to resurrect and maintain the Confederate section of Oakwood Cemetery. Their contribution to history is something anyone who reveres, respects and honors their Confederate, Southern heritage or those who value history in general can appreciate. This book is a way to thank them and recognize their hard work.

— *Frank B. Powell, III*
Editor

A Story Behind Every Stone

The main Confederate Monument which was erected in 1867.

A Story Behind Every Stone   v

The House of Memory in 2004.

A Story Behind Every Stone

Introduction

The continuing work in the Confederate Section of Oakwood Cemetery in Raleigh, North Carolina, has been and continues to be a labor of love and teamwork for more than 140 years.

The Ladies Memorial Association of Wake County began the effort in 1866 by planning, securing a plot of land and reinterring the bodies of Confederate Soldiers in and around Wake County. After the soldiers were placed in the Soldiers' Cemetery (Oakwood Cemetery Association was not formed until 1869), the ladies kept up the work of replacing wooden headboards with granite markers. They kept up the grounds and planted new bushes and flowers. They helped in the care of the old soldiers in the Old Soldiers' Home. They brought back soldiers buried in Gettysburg and Arlington Cemeteries and had them buried in Oakwood.

After the Ladies Memorial Association disbanded in 1919, the Johnston Pettigrew Chapter of the United Daughters of the Confederacy took up the task of keeping up the Confederate section. As the old soldiers died in the home and were buried in Oakwood, the Pettigrew Chapter (as the Ladies Memorial Association before them) kept up with ordering and placing a numbered stone for each of the soldiers. Later the House of Memory was built under the direction of Mrs. Alfred Williams. Mrs. Frances Hoffman was for many years in charge of supervising the work in the Soldiers' Cemetery.

"During the years constant and untiring care has been exercised, not only to keep the grounds in order, but to make them more beautiful." Stated Mrs. Hoffman in a report. Many graves had to be refilled, hundreds of pounds of grass seed were sown, and flowers were planted in profusion (irises, daffodils, roses, wisteria and trees.) This work was carried on till the late 1970s.

Beginning in the late 1980s, local camps of the Sons of Confederate Veterans picked up the mantle in restoring Oakwood. The Oakwood Restoration Project was formed and soon the members were busy researching the Oakwood Soldiers — their full names, rank, dates of birth and death, military unit and any other information that would help in telling the story of each soldier. The new project included cleaning and restoring the monuments, as well as stopping the erosion of the grounds. In less than a year they began to erect government headstones for the soldiers. This task took ten and a half years to complete.

The business now is to easily identify the location of the soldiers and make this available to the current and future descendants of Confederate soldiers buried among the almost 1,400 men in the Soldiers' Section.

In the beginning of the 21st century, the Sons replaced the Speaker's Pavilion (or Gazebo) which was destroyed by Hurricane Fran in 1996, erected two site maps and continued in identifying those with *Unknown Soldier* headstones.

This labor of love and teamwork through generations has worked well, and it is the desire of all that it continues, as long as it takes, to bring recognition of each man, his due.

A Story Behind Every Stone

A view of Oakwood from sometime in the 1930s.

The House of Memory in 1936.

A Story Behind Every Stone

This 1873 photo shows wooden markers identifying the graves.

Numbered granite stones marked the graves when the restoration project started.

A Story Behind Every Stone

The Work Behind the Oakwood Confederate Cemetery

In 1853 the first North Carolina State Fair was begun east of the Capitol building on Tarboro Avenue. When the war started in 1861, this location was turned into the Fairground Hospital for Confederate Soldiers. When the soldiers died in the Fairground Hospital in the first year they were buried in Raleigh's City Cemetery (until mid-summer 1862). They were then buried near the Fairground Hospital in the Rock Quarry Cemetery (now Raleigh National Cemetery).

At the conclusion of the war, the Union Army chose this same cemetery for laying their dead in graves from the battlefields of Aversboro and Bentonville, also from the hospital cemeteries of Goldsboro, Raleigh and Greensboro, plus other small sites in between. Soon they had to move the Confederate Soldiers to another location.

The Ladies Memorial Association of Wake County was organized May 23, 1866, with a priority to "consecrate some spot sacred to our heroic dead." Later that summer, Mr. P. F. Pescud and Mr. George Mordecai requested land from Mr. Henry Mordecai for this purpose. Evidently they had made some financial offer, to which Mr. Henry Mordecai replied, "Mr. Pescud, the Ladies Memorial Association are welcome to as many acres of my land as the need for such a sacred purpose."

A plan of the grounds was submitted by Mr. Pescue on February 24, 1867, resulting in "the first Confederate Cemetery in the late Confederacy of which [Mr. Pescue] has any knowledge." The deed to "the Soldier's Cemetery" is dated March 19, 1867. It was in the mind of Miss Sophia Partridge — a lady distinguished for her purity, refinement, and sympathetic nature, that the thought originated, and an association for the reinterment and future care of the dead heroes first dawned. It is her influence and persistent exertions that led to the first Confederate Cemetery in the late Confederacy.

After clearing trees and stumps, the tremendous task of moving 546 Confederate dead from gravesites in many areas of Wake County began. From the Rock Quarry Cemetery (now the National Cemetery of Raleigh) came 494 Confederate bodies. All were identified using wooden board bearing their names and states and in most cases, their military units.

The following is a list of events toward the inception and completion of the Oakwood Restoration project, with full and honorable recognition of the deceased Confederate soldier. Lest we forget.

On February 14, 1867, the North Carolina Legislature appropriated $1,500 for the erection of a Confederate Monument in the Confederate Cemetery.

On May 10, 1867, the first observance of the Confederate dead was held at the Soldiers' cemetery.

In June 1868, Mr. Watson took the first known photograph of the Confederate Cemetery.

The main Oakwood Cemetery was chartered in 1869, and many citizens of Raleigh removed their dead from the old city cemetery to Oakwood. In 1870, the earliest Hebrew Cemetery was established in a space between the Confederate and Oakwood cemeteries.

In February 1870, the first veteran, Captain George M. Whiting, was buried in the Soldiers' Section of Oakwood.

In 1871, 137 bodies were brought from Gettysburg and reburied on August 25, 1871, in separate graves.

In 1877, the rotting wood headboards were replaced with granite stones, each with a number chiseled on top corresponding to a paper roster list.

A Speaker's Pavilion or Summer House was erected in 1881. A Confederate bazaar was held to raise money for this purpose.

On March 11, 1881, the North Carolina General Assembly made May 10 a legal Confederate holiday.

In October 1883, 107 soldiers from Arlington Cemetery were

reinterred in Oakwood.

April 14, 1896, the General Pettigrew Chapter of the United Daughters of the Confederacy was formed in Raleigh.

The Memorial Gateway was unveiled on May 10, 1910, by the Pettigrew Chapter.

By 1919, most of the members of the Ladies Memorial Association of Wake Country had passed away. As the remaining members were also in the Johnston Pettigrew Chapter of the United Daughter of the Confederacy, the two organizations were merged on February 27, 1919, and the UDC took responsibility for the cemetery and memorial services. The Ladies Memorial Association of Raleigh passed out of existence, having served for fifty-three years in honoring the memory of North Carolina's Confederate soldiers.

In 1930, a Memorial Brick Wall was built on the south side of the Confederate section on Oakwood Avenue, containing 52,000 bricks.

In the spring of 1935, only sixteen soldiers of the Confederacy remained in the Soldiers' Home in Raleigh.

On October 15, 1935, the Memorial Pavilion, The House of Memory, was dedicated to all North Carolinians who have fought and died for their country on land and sea. The stone pavilion stands to the west of the Confederate cemetery, on a slope overlooking a small valley and creek. Dr. Frank P. Graham, president of the University of North Carolina, delivered an address declaring that "a land without memories is a land without hope." The cost of the pavilion was $4,427.93.

On May 10, 1936, the first Memorial Day exercise at The House of Memory was held.

During the Christmas period of 1936, there were only seven elderly veterans in the Soldiers' Home in the hospital ward.

On June 21, 1938, the last veteran from the old soldier's home was buried in the Soldier's Cemetery in Oakwood. Several have been reinterred since then and the only lady (Mrs. William Burgwyn) was buried beside her husband in 1941.

In the spring of 1988, three Sons of Confederate Veterans members — Jeff Morton, Charles Purser and Thomas Smith (chairman) — formed the Oakwood Restoration Project. It was a plan to research the soldiers' identities, order government headstones and erect the stones in the Soldiers' Cemetery.

In June/July 1988, the research began.

With permission from the Pettigrew Chapter, the first eleven headstones with each soldier's name, rank, unit, date of birth (if known) and engraved death date were erected January 15, 1990.

An unknown North Carolinian Confederate soldier's remains found near the Cold Harbor, VA, battlefield was reinterred in Oakwood on October 28, 1990.

On May 2, 1993, a large memorial marker of the Arlington dead was placed over their mass graves. This marker states the soldiers' name, rank, unit and dates of birth/death.

On September 6, 1996, the Oakwood project had a six-month setback after Hurricane Fran devastated the area and the cemetery. The Speaker's Pavilion was completely destroyed. Four giant oaks (more than two hundred years old) and other smaller

Just one of the downed trees after Hurricane Fran.

trees came down on the graves, tossing many up in the air and driving others more than two feet into the waterlogged ground. After all was put back in place, none of the headstones had to be replaced.

A Story Behind Every Stone

North Carolina's Unknown Confederate Soldier.

During North Carolina Memorial Day in May 1997, a monument was unveiled at the head of the Gettysburg section, with an inscription explaining how these soldiers were moved.

In August 2000, the last government headstone was erected in Oakwood. **"It is one of the hopes and dreams of the United Daughters of the Confederacy to mark the graves with a government marker"** wrote Mrs. A. W. Hoffman in the 1970s. She was the UDC chairman of the State Confederate Cemetery in Raleigh committee.

In 2004, cornerstones for each of the cemetery's eight divisions were placed.

In 2006, two informational site maps were erected for the many visitors to the Confederate Cemetery.

On May 6, 2006, a new Speaker's Pavilion was dedicated using the original plans of the old Pavilion.

On September 23, 2007, a headstone for the first Union Soldier discovered in the Gettysburg section was unveiled. Also on this date, two headstones of newly identified Confederate Soldiers were unveiled replacing the *Unknown Soldier* status.

On May 3, 2008, during the Confederate Memorial Service, five new headstones were unveiled with the identity of previously *Unknown Soldiers.*

On August 9, 2008, a headstone for the second Union Soldier discovered in the Gettysburg section was unveiled.

On May 1, 2010, during the Confederate Memorial Service, three new headstones were unveiled with the identity of previously *Unknown Soldiers.*

A view of the cemetery looking towards the House of Memory.

A Story Behind Every Stone

The Confederate Hospitals of Raleigh and Wake County

After the outbreak of the war, Raleigh quickly emerged as an important medical center for the Confederacy. The city was strategically located along the rail lines which carried troops to and from Virginia, and Raleigh was removed enough from the front to be safe from enemy incursions.

North Carolina's first military hospital, known as the Fair Grounds Hospital, was opened in Raleigh in May 1861, under the direction of Dr. Edmund Burke Haywood. This site was the location of the North Carolina State Fair, which began in 1853. The installation served as a receiving hospital for a large camp of instruction. Hospital records from May 20, 1861, to August 1, 1862 — when it was taken over by the Confederate government and redesignated General Hospital No. 7 — show 4,731 patients were admitted for treatment. In the duration of its operation, the Fairground center lost only 229 out of 6,916 patients admitted, and returned 5,894 to duty. In the first year, the dead were buried in the Raleigh City Cemetery. Outbreaks of contagious diseases such as pneumonia and measles among the camps routinely kept the hospital filled and accounted for many deaths during the first two years of the war.

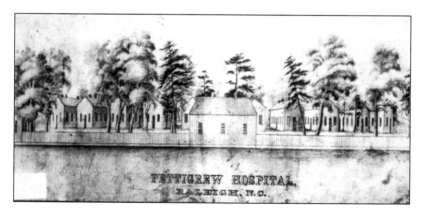

The unfinished main hall of Peace Institute was chosen as the site of General Hospital No. 8, in the spring of 1862. Dr. Thomas H. Hill rushed to prepare the three-story facility to receive the first patients, and by June, 1862, work had progressed to a stage

An unidentified veteran leaves the Soldiers' Home on his way to a United Confederate Veterans' Reunion.

A Story Behind Every Stone

where the hospital could be opened. As glass was unavailable, window frames were covered with painted cloth to keep out the elements. Dr. Hill was relieved after its opening, and Dr. H. G. Leigh directed the hospital until the close of the war.

In June 1864, Dr. Haywood took charge of the largest military hospital in Raleigh, the newly constructed Pettigrew Hospital (General Hospital No. 13). The facility was located on the present site of the Division of Motor Vehicles on the southwest side of New Bern Avenue and Tarboro Streets and adjacent to the north side of General Hospital No. 7. This hospital was named in honor of General James J. Pettigrew, mortally wounded in the retreat from Gettysburg the previous year. Like Peace Hospital, Pettigrew Hospital was not completed when opened; but as the only facility built in Raleigh solely for medical use, it featured its own dispensary, laundry, kitchen and mess, stable, bath house and guard house. It had beds for 400 patients. In the years 1892 to 1938, this site was the location of the Old Soldiers' Home and currently is the location of North Carolina's Department of Motor Vehicals headquarters.

The proximity of Wake Forest College to the Raleigh-Gaston Railroad was an important consideration in establishing a general hospital there. As with Peace Institute, the main hall was appropriated for hospital use in June 1864. Dr. J. G. Broadnax was appointed director.

The approach of General William T. Sherman near the war's end created considerable turmoil in Raleigh's hospital system. Casualties poured in after the battles of Averasboro and Bentonville in March 1865, completely overwhelming the local general hospitals. Private homes, hotels and churches contained the overflow. Most of the Confederate cemetery's dead from other states fell mortally wounded during these engagements and were transported to Raleigh.

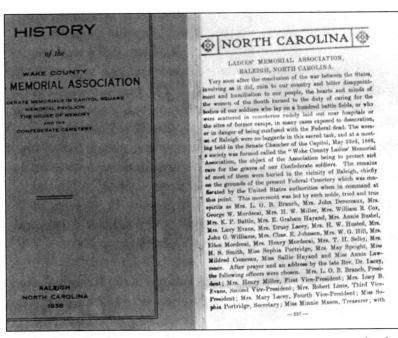

An early history of the Ladies Memorial Association in Raleigh.

A Story Behind Every Stone

Disinterring and Reinterring the Bodies of Our Dead
by
The Ladies Memorial Association of Raleigh, NC

Prepared by P. F. Pescud, 1882

I t was in the mind of Miss Sophia Partridge, a lady distinguished for her purity, refinement and sympathetic nature, that the thought originated, an association for the reinterment and future care of our dead heroes first dawned, and it is to her influence and persistent exertions that the first Confederate Cemetery in the late Confederacy of which the writer has any knowledge, was organized.

After devoting an hour or two every day for several weeks to a survey of the suburbs of the city, the premises now occupied and known as the Ladies Memorial Cemetery was agreed upon. This land was owned by Mr. Henry Mordeci and the gentleman knew that the writer had for years, as a member of the city council in vain advocated the necessity for a larger and more suitable cemetery than the old one on Hargett Street.

When therefore, in company with George W. Mordecai, he asked Mr. Henry Mordecai to make a donation of as many acres as the ladies wanted, and as an inducement for such liberality agreed to raise a joint stock company to purchase his land adjoining, and to convert it into a cemetery park, the generous Mordecai replied: "Mr. Pescud, the Ladies Memorial Association are welcome to as many acres of my land as they need for such a sacred purpose, without any consideration, and not only this, but concerning the enterprise you refer to, and which has been so long on your heart, I will aid you to the extent of my ability in the price of the land wanted for that purpose."

The late George W. Whiting was chairman of the committee to ascertain where our fallen heroes were buried and to have their

The earliest known photograph, June 1868, of the Confederate section of Oakwood Cemetery. All the headstones are wooden.

remains disinterred and removed to the cemetery. He, assisted by Misses Blanch Bragg, Annie Lovejoy and Sue B. Pescud, remarked in pencil all the headboards at the graves they found and prepared a list of the names before the graves were opened. Mr. P.F. Pescud, aided by the ladies, received and superintended the reinterment of the remains, which work was begun 22nd of February, 1867, and occupied several weeks. After this a large number of ladies (old and young) made a selection of graves to be adorned with flowers on anniversary occasions and at intermediate times. This practice is still observed, especially by those who assisted in nursing or carrying delicacies to the deceased during their last illness. These graves are distinguished by flowers and shrubbery near them, and the turning which is kept fresh.

It is in this connection, proper to mention, that we were forced to reinter the remains of our noble soldiers before the cem-

A Story Behind Every Stone

etery was in readiness, because of the heartlessness of the wretch sent by the authorities at Washington City to prepare a cemetery for the Federal dead, in which confiscated ground interred most of our dead. The said *Nero* sent insulting messages to the Memorial Association, insisting on the removal of the Confederate dead before the cemetery was in readiness for the graves to be opened and finally threatened that if our dead were not removed by a given day, their remains would be placed in the public road. This inhuman conduct moved our ex-Confederates and youth to the front. With commendable alacrity, they responded to the call of the ladies. Stimulated by their presence and smiles, day after day, with zeal commensurate with their reverence for the remains of their late companions in arms, and sympathy in the labor of love the dear women had begun, they undertook the task of disinterring and reinterring our dead, and labored until all the bodies found in or near this city were deposited in the Confederate Cemetery. When informed of his conduct the commandant of this post severely rebuked the man in charge of the Federal cemetery, and on the following anniversary with his family, brought a large quantity of rare flowers to the cemetery, stood uncovered in front of the orator during the delivery of his address, and then placed the flowers over graves of our dead.

The Memorial Gateway was unveiled on May 10, 1910, by the James Johnston Pettigrew Chapter of the UDC.

A Story Behind Every Stone

The Confederate Cemetery, Raleigh, North Carolina

When the Ladies Memorial Association of Wake County was organized May 23, 1866, one of their first objectives was to find a suitable spot for 'our heroic dead'. Mr. Henry Mordecai told Mr. P. F. Pescud after a request for land with a financial offer, "Mr. Pescud, the Ladies Memorial Association is welcome to as many acres of my land as they need for such a sacred purpose."

A plan for the grounds submitted by Mr. Pescud resulted in "the first Confederate Cemetery in the late Confederacy of which Mr. Pescud has any knowledge." The deed to "Soldier's Cemetery" is dated March, 1867. The tremendous task of moving 546 bodies of the Confederate dead from sites in many areas of Wake County was preceded by clearing trees and stumps and otherwise putting the donated land in proper condition.

The cemetery was laid off in eight divisions with the first four numbered designated for North Carolinians. Division 5 was delegated for the 44 Georgia dead, Division 6 for the nine from Mississippi, Division 7 has four rows of South Carolina soldiers and Division 8 contained 106 unknowns, plus 70 soldiers from most of the remaining States.

George W. Whiting was chairman of the committee to ascertain where the soldiers were buried and to have their remains disinterred and removed to the cemetery. He, assisted by Misses Blanch Bragg, Annie Lovejoy and Sue B. Pescud, remarked in pencil all the headboards at the graves they found, and prepared a list of the names before the graves were opened. Mr. Pescud and the ladies received and superintended the reinterment of the remains. The work was begun February 22, 1867, and occupied several weeks.

Most of the Confederate dead in Wake County were buried during the war in Rock Quarry Cemetery, just across the road from the old Fairgrounds Hospital and the Pettigrew Hospital (later the Soldier's Home). When the Federal Army came to Raleigh, they took possession of the hospitals and the cemetery. A Federal officer in command of the cemetery selected it for the interment of their own dead and sent word to the mayor of the city that bodies must be removed as they desired that spot for the burial of their own dead. A later threat was supposedly verbalized that if the Confederate soldiers buried there were not removed in two days, their bodies would be thrown in the road.

The threat stirred to activity all the loyal citizens of the town, and preparations sped up for their removal to the Soldiers' Cemetery, even while the grounds were being prepared. The work was done almost entirely by young men of the city who fought side by side with their fellow comrades, a labor of love. With picks and wheelbarrows they were assisted by women relatives walking by their side. In that early day, 1867, they moved 494 from Rock Quarry Cemetery, 20 from the city cemetery, 14 near Henry Mordecai's, eight from Wake Forest, six from Camp Mangum (current site of the State Fair and Meredith College), two from Camp Holmes, and one each from Chapel Hill (a young Alabama lad), Mrs. Price's farm and Flowlet's farm (last two locations currently unknown).

In 1871, 137 bodies were removed from Gettysburg and reinterred in the Soldiers' Cemetery. In 1883, 107 dead were removed from National Cemetery at Arlington and laid to rest in two mass graves in Oakwood. Beginning in the late 1880s, veterans from the Soldiers' Home were transferred to the cemetery. In 2010, there are 1,388 Confederate and two Union Soldiers buried in the Soldiers' Cemetery in Oakwood.

A Story Behind Every Stone

*Two old soldiers pose for a photo in front of one of the buildings
on the Soldiers' Home campus.*

Colonel Henry King Burgwyn, the boy colonel of the Confederacy, killed on the first day of the battle at Gettysburg.

A Story Behind Every Stone

The Gettysburg Dead

After the Confederate surrender in 1865, various Ladies Memorial Associations began to appear throughout the Southern states. Their focus was to locate and identify Confederate gravesites and then make sure they were properly maintained and their dead and the sites honored. These groups universally believed that Confederate soldiers buried in Pennsylvania were among a hostile populace who viewed them as traitors.

The Ladies Memorial Associations of several states began to contract for the removal of their respective dead to be shipped back for reinterment. In North Carolina, the Wake County Ladies Memorial Association decided in the summer of 1871 to initiate the task of removing their state's dead from Gettysburg.

These remains were scattered over a large area. Those who were killed in action or died of wounds before they could be taken to a hospital were buried on the field by their comrades. Many of those wounded/sick and captured died in the Union's General Letterman Hospital, located on the grounds. Just after the battle there were more than 60 small hospitals with more than 20,000 Union and Confederate wounded all over the battlefield (5,456 Confederates in twenty-four of those hospital camps). By the end of July 1863, 16,125 wounded had been sent away from Gettysburg and approximately 4,217, unfit to travel, were placed in the Letterman Hospital. The two lower rows next to the House of Memory are the graves of the Letterman Hospital patients. A few died on the retreat to Virginia.

The work of exhuming, boxing and shipping North Carolina's dead was handled by Dr. Rufus B. Weaver. Dr. Weaver's efforts supplemented the work of his father, Samuel Weaver of Gettysburg, who had helped catalogue hundreds of marked Confederate graves and their location. The sites of several thousand unknown soldiers were also identified by their burial locations and the pe-

*The monument marking the Gettysburg dead
section was dedicated in May 1997.*

culiarities of the uniforms on the corpses, which varied so much-
from those worn by Union soldiers. Dr. Weaver's specialization
in anatomy enabled his identification of many sets of remains,
particularly when hospital records were available to categorize
wound types suffered by individual soldiers. As gunshot wounds
commonly resulted in amputation, for example, records citing
such surgery were of immense importance in identifying skeletal
remains.

On August 25, 1871, 137 sets of remains were shipped by Dr.
Weaver to Raleigh, which were reinterred in the southwest area of
the Confederate section of Oakwood Cemetery. These included
119 identified remains, which were buried in individual graves,
four identified remains in a mass grave (all members of the 6th
North Carolina Infantry), and 14 unknowns buried in another
mass grave (all of Iverson's Brigade). One South Carolinian and
two Virginians were mistakenly returned, also, but they were
reinterred along with the other soldiers' remains. Another Virgin-

A Story Behind Every Stone

ian, Captain William W. McCreery, a West Pointer on General Pettigrew's Staff, was one of the fourteen flag bearers of the 26th North Carolina shot down during a charge on the first day at Gettysburg. He was buried among the 26th and came home with them. To these Gettysburg dead must be added six soldiers who were mortally wounded at Gettysburg but transported to Raleigh through the hospital system — only to die in Raleigh. The Confederate section of Oakwood Cemetery thus contains 143 Gettysburg dead, some nine percent of the approximately 1,600 North Carolina soldiers who died during that campaign.

One hundred and twenty-six years later, the Sons of Confederate Veterans placed a large Gettysburg Memorial at the head of the Gettysburg section.

During 2007-08, extensive research identified two of the Gettysburg dead as Federal Soldiers. One was a sharpshooter from Minnesota while the other was a German born New York City soldier.

A plaque in the House of Memory erroneously lists 2,800 soldiers buried in the Confederate section of Oakwood. There are actually only 1,390 soldiers buried in the Confederate section, but more are buried throughout the rest of the cemetery.

Arlington Dead

During the latter part of September 1883, the Ladies Memorial Association made arrangements to have the North Carolina soldiers buried at Arlington Cemetery returned home. For nineteen long years these soldiers have lain in an almost secluded spot in the Federal cemetery at Arlington, their graves marked by a simple pine board with the inscription, **N.C. Rebel.** In the first week of October 1883, the remains were disinterred and brought to Alexandria, Virginia, by undertaker Wheatley, where they were placed in four caskets for shipment to Raleigh.

The caskets, under an honor guard, moved through the principal streets of Alexandria to the wharf, where they were conveyed to the steamer *George Leary*. Free transportation was furnished by the Potomac steamboat company which included their escorts' fee to ride. When they arrived at Norfolk, Virginia, they were met by The Norfolk Light Artillery Blues, The Norfolk City Guard and old Confederate soldiers.

The procession passed many thousands of people lining the streets, especially ladies bearing flowers. The bells tolled, and all the flags on all the ships in port, on public buildings and on the United States Custom House were half-mast. They wound slowly along the streets to impressive music played by the band from the Soldiers' Home.

On arrival in Portsmouth, the procession was met by the Old Dominion Guards, the Confederate veterans and the Ladies Memorial Association. During the passage by the ferry, minute-guns were fired by Chambers Battery. The caskets were transferred to the Seaboard & Roanoke Railroad. On their entrance to Suffolk, they found the Suffolk Grays in line, awaiting their arrival.

Upon arrival in Raleigh on October 16th, the remains were transported under a large escort to the Capitol, where they laid in state over night under constant guard of the Raleigh Light Infantry. All through the night, there were visitors to the building. Early in the morning the Fayetteville Independent Light Infantry took charge as guard of honor. The bank of flowers over the caskets grew larger by the hour.

Early in the afternoon of the 17th, the procession of troops and dignitaries began to form in front of the court house, promptly, and began its march up Fayetteville Street to the Capitol. On arrival at the Capitol square, the Raleigh Light Infantry and the Bingham cadets brought the caskets out the east side and placed them in the funeral car. After the usual ceremonies the line of march was taken to the cemetery. Along the way the streets were lined with people, while at the cemetery hundreds gathered.

With the military drawn up on three sides of a square, they rendered the salute and the band then played a dirge. Then Governor Jarvis stepped into the centre of the square and spoke in clear and ringing tones, heard far and near. Calling them "patriot soldiers," he said that as these comrades went forth in 1861 at the command of their State and of the Governor of North Carolina — the Governor of the State should today receive them back and speak for the State in so doing. The address was heard with the closest attention. In all that assemblage of five thousand persons not a sound was heard.

The four caskets containing the remains were laid in two graves immediately south of the Confederate monument. Volleys were fired over the graves, after which the full honors of a marching salute were paid as the troops filed past. Over the two graves were placed two markers inscribed with the word *Arlington.*

One hundred and ten years later on May 2, 1993, the Sons of Confederate Veterans erected a 2-ton granite marker over their resting place. The bronze plate on the granite had the names, rank, dates and units of 102 soldiers, with five unknowns (ten years later two of the five unknowns have been identified and a

A Story Behind Every Stone

The Arlington monument which was dedicated on May 2, 1993.

small granite marker was placed to them at the base of the large granite). The honor guard at the mass grave was provided by the Fayetteville Independent Light Infantry. The same unit present in 1883 when the remains were reintered.

A close-up view of the Confederate Soldier's Home in Raleigh. The two mortars are now at Fort Macon, NC.

A Story Behind Every Stone

Soldiers' Home

The North Carolina Confederate Soldier's Home as it stood in 1910.

In October 1889, the Confederate Veteran Association adopted a resolution that a home for helpless, disabled veterans was a necessity. By August 29 of the following year, about $3,000 in money and good notes had been secured for this purpose. The property at the corner of Polk and Bloodworth Streets was rented at a cost of $12.50 per month, and was soon filled to overflowing. The Legislature, by an act passed February 16, 1891, appropriated $3,000 per annum, and donated what is known as the Camp Russell Property, located on the southwest corner of New Bern and Tarboro Street (the General Pettigrew Hospital No. 13 location). It consisted of about five acres of land, and a lot of undressed pine board tumble-down old buildings.

In 1892 and 1893, two additional buildings were erected for a dining room and a laundry, plus a hospital. Sixty-five inmates were comfortably accommodated. A system of rules and regulations were introduced, and persistent violation of rules by any inmates met with discharge.

In 1900, a large hospital and then in 1902 a large dormitory consisting of twenty-four rooms, including reception rooms, offices, etc., were added, which accommodated fifty additional men. At this time there were 110 on the roll and in the next several years the numbers stayed in the 110 – 150 range. The State appropriated $13,000 annually for the maintenance of the institution. The greatest enrollments were reached in 1917, with 209 inmates and 188 inmates in 1919. The largest yearly appropriations for the home came in 1920, and the enrollment dropped to 93 inmates in 1926.

In May, 1935, there were only sixteen soldiers of the Confederacy being cared for at the Soldiers' Home in Raleigh. At this time, instead of the large dining room which in former years seated as many as 150 veterans, there is now a smaller room, containing three tables, each of which seats six. Of the eleven buildings, only three are in use. The hospital building is now the center for most of the activities of the members.

The last resident left to live with friends in 1938, and was placed on the pension roll with the other 180 veterans who were receiving a pension from North Carolina. The home closed in August 1938 and the buildings were used by the National Youth Administration and the Raleigh Recreation Commission until 1940, at which time most of the buildings were torn down. The North Carolina Department of Motor Vehicles is currently located on this site.

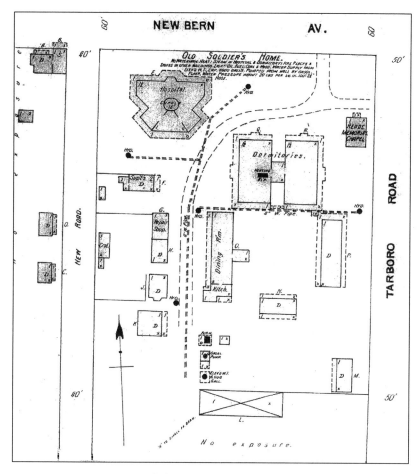

1903 Map of the Confederate Soldier's Home.

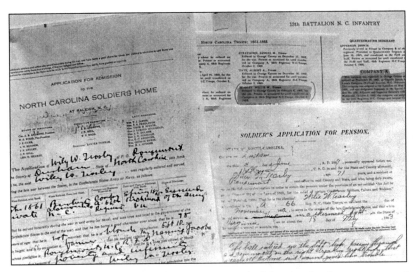

Examples of some of the documents and old records that were used in the research of the cemetery.

A Story Behind Every Stone

The Research

When the Oakwood headstone project began in the spring of 1988, the research team of Jeff Morton, Charles Purser and Hunter Edwards had little information to help with the research. Jeff and Charles' first task was to survey every stone in the Confederate section. After the survey and after plotting the results on a large board, a 1914 survey map was discovered in the North Carolina Archives map section. This helped confirm the numbering system in place at that time, which actually was three different numbering systems depending on the death date. More than two dozen numbered stones were missing, but a search in the ground found them buried, as much as two feet below ground level. Also, with the help of Bryon Brady, a 1914 typewritten listing of the soldiers in Oakwood became our main source in the research. This list had no ranks or births listed, and incomplete names or units as well as missing years (1888-1898) on the first fifty veterans buried in the cemetery. The 1914 map indicated several unmarked graves. After probing with a long rod, we were able to confirm the locations.

The research began with completing the easily identified soldiers with their military records and census records. This style of research became the norm, working the documented soldiers first and putting the harder to identify on hold. Soon we ordered the first dozen or so marble headstones from the Veterans Administration. Later, the VA bypassed the required attachments of proof after we submitted documentations on ten soldiers in all parts of the cemetery. They just wanted to check if we knew what we were doing.

Our first markers arrived at a business on South Saunders Street in Raleigh. On the first workday in Oakwood on Saturday, January 15, 1990, the volunteer crew with pickups loaded the markers and took them to the awaiting members at the cemetery.

We soon realized that this arrangement would not work and began talking with the Oakwood Cemetery staff about the logistics of receiving the markers and having them in place on workdays. This arrangement stayed in place for the next ten years. We would order from ten to fifty markers at a time in order to have them on hand for the anxious volunteers on the Saturday after the second Tuesday (the meeting night of the Garner, NC, Sons of Confederate Veterans).

The Confederate list grew as research continued. The research team corresponded with out-of-state archives, other SCV groups, the UDC, the National Archives, a retired New York policeman who is an expert on North Carolinians at Gettysburg, county historians (in and out of state). They poured over records at the North Carolina Archives, the Oakwood Cemetery books, the UNC Wilson Library, Duke University, local newspapers (during and after the war), books at the NC State University library, Wake County Health Department and the Wake County Library.

A problem became apparent with the lack of names for the stones from 1914 to 1924. The typed list contained only names up to 1914. The cemetery records had their list in the beginning, but became lax at the duty until a new superintendent started recording the veterans buried in the Confederate section in 1924. We had two hundred stones in that ten-year span, with numbers stamped in them, but no list of names. Jeff and Charles, with the permission of the Wake County Health Department, searched every name in death certificates of people who died in Wake County from the years 1914 to 1924. They looked for any veteran who died in the soldiers' home and was buried in Oakwood. This system worked fine — they came up with 201 names. Using death-date order, Charles then assigned a vet to a stone, with the extra one going to an open spot.

The typed list also contained the names of two veterans with the same number. These two names stayed on hold until the cemetery staff found a paper in the back of their safe. Of the two names, the first vet was buried for only a few years, when his family decided they wanted him back home. At that time, the next vet who died in the soldiers' home was buried in the open grave evidently to save the work of having him next in line.

In the late 1990s, the fast growing advancement of the research material on the Internet helped in the correct identification of several soldiers. By the year 2010, approximately 56 soldiers with partial information have not been found in any military records. They may not be found due to reading the rotting wooden markers in 1877, conscripts not yet entered on any unit records or they could be from other states. The asterisk '*' in front of their names in the Alpha list indicates that their headstone has *Unknown Soldier*, but the written list shows what little information noted for that soldier. The hope is that in the future better computers, more available data or better minds will identify these soldiers.

A view of the Summer House in the early 1990s before Hurricane Fran toppled the large Oak tree on top of it. The flagpole and large Confederate Monument were spared.

A Story Behind Every Stone

Oakwood Confederate
Cemetery Restoration Committee
(Goals and Logistics)
by Thomas M. Smith, Chairman

It was in late 1988 that members from the Colonel Henry King Burgwyn Jr. Camp 1485 and the Leonidas LaFayette Polk Camp 1486 met, and upon a request/recommendation by North Carolina Division Sons of Confederate Veterans Commander Byron Brady, formed a committee which was to work closely with the United Daughters of the Confederacy to maintain, restore and replace the old markers with new Veterans Administration markers. Later these intentions grew into an overall project of restoration and maintenance throughout the cemetery.

Most graves were marked with small, square granite stones with corresponding numbers. These numbers were becoming faint and sometimes hard-to-read, not to overlook that names, birth and death dates as well as regiment and companies were not mentioned. Now, all graves are marked with veterans markers bearing the soldier's name, dates and unit numbers. Under each 230-pound stone a forty-pound bag of concrete was placed to act as a footing. Committee workdays continue today in straightening, cleaning and leveling out these markers. The marker installation portion of the restoration effort has been completed. Now, almost 1,400 gravesites are marked.

Landscaping concerns in the beginning were also a potential problem for the committee. Since the cemetery is on a huge hill, erosion has been a continuous problem. One of our first efforts was to haul in several dumptruck-loads of topsoil and spread it out over the hillside. Grass seed and plugs were planted and then fertilized and limed. The canopy of some of the larger oak trees was raised by trimming the lower branches, letting more sunlight in to aid in growing a proper groundcover. Over the years, and through funding resulting from our annual Lantern Walk each fall, brick-paved walkways are being installed, replacing uneven and dangerous rock paths as well as an old concrete sidewalk that had been broken and pushed up by the roots of hundred-year-old oak trees. More walkways are planned, as well as a comprehensive landscape plan.

The House of Memory, which was built in 1935, is situated on the lower portion of the lot. This structure originally had a flat roof with an internal guttering system. Due to constant leaking problems, a wooden shed roof was added on in the 1950s. Due to the added stress caused by the weight of the new shed roof, one of the limestone arches burst and was missing for many years. Through a grant and private fundraising, the missing arch was replaced in the last decade. The shed roof was removed and a rubber membrane placed back. The internal guttering system was reworked. The restoration committee hopes to one day tackle numerous other problems with this structure. The slate floor needs reworking. The bronze plaques, which are dedicated to all North Carolina veterans in all wars, need to be cleaned professionally. In a report by then-chairman of this State Confederate Cemetery, Mrs. A.W. Hoffman states concerning the House of Memory, "There the visitor to the Confederate Cemetery may find shelter from the sun and rain and inspiration to contemplate the glories and heroics of past years."

On the night of September 5, 1996, during Hurricane Fran, the cemetery suffered a major lost when one of the two-hundred-year-old oak trees came crashing down on the Speaker's Pavilion. The pavilion, also known as the Summer House, was dedicated in 1881 and was the site of many memorable lectures and speeches during the last century. Pieces of this historical structure were found more than a hundred yards away the next day. These pieces were put into storage until 2006 when they were used as samples to duplicate as closely as possible the original structure. Because of the fund-raising efforts of then Cemetery Board of Directors

President John C. Williams and many Sons of Confederate Veteran members and camps, the replacement pavilion was dedicated on May 6, 2006. After the structure went up a new section of the brick walkway was added. The new section of walkway extended from the main front gate on Oakwood Avenue to and around the Speaker's Pavilion and then on to the General Anderson Monument. This section of walkway is referred to as *The Walk of Honor* and contains hundreds of personalized bricks.

The Wall of Memory, which was built in the 1930s, is crumbling in some areas and is in need of refurbishing. This wall is on the Oakwood Avenue side and is responsible for holding tons of cemetery soil in place. Another future item, which needs attention, is the main Confederate Monument. This giant structure is made of soft white marble. It was installed and dedicated in 1870 and is one of the first Confederate Monuments in the state. It is held together with iron clamps from the inside; which have apparently rusted away. The top portion, weighing so much, has pushed the sides out exposing the original quarry marks on the cut stone. This structure will one day need to be disassembled and reassembled.

This project continues to be a labor of love by those who have dedicated themselves to the memory of Southern honor and historical accuracy. The cemetery is listed on the National Historic Registery. The committee's efforts are solely that of restoration, and only by using historical notes as our pattern. This committee, which is structured under the Sons of Confederate Veterans, has a symbiotic relationship with Oakwood Cemetery Association to further brighten the future of this sacred ground. We are thankful for their dedication to history and all they continue to do. We also would like to thank the United Daughters of the Confederacy. Without their foresight many years ago, this cemetery might not have been established. We look forward to the future with expectations of maintaining and preserving one of the most beautiful military cemeteries in existence today.

Four Confederate veterans in one of the reading rooms at the Soldiers' Home.

A Story Behind Every Stone

A Sampling of Stories Behind the Stones

Captain William Westwood McCreey (son of George Magee McCreery & Matilda Werth McCreery) graduated at West Point as second lieutenant of artillery in 1860: resigned to serve in the Confederate Army; killed at Gettysburg, July 1, 1863, age 27, in Pettigrew's Division. He often had said that should he fall in battle he would like to be color bearer at the time; his wish was granted, as he fell on the breast works, being the tenth of fourteen men killed or wounded while bearing the flag of the 26th NC.

Colonel Wallace Bruce Colbert of Leake County, Mississippi, voted on January 9, 1861 for the *Ordinance of Secession* for the state of Mississippi. He organized the 40th Mississippi at Meridian, MS. Colonel Colbert was mortally wounded while leading the 40th Mississippi Infantry in the last gallant Confederate charge of the war at Bentonville, North Carolina, on March 19, 1865.

Colonel Henry King Burgwyn, Jr. was born near Boston, Massachusetts, at the home of his mother's parents, on October 3, 1841. His formative years were spent on his family's plantation, Thornberry, in Northampton County, NC. He attended the Virginia Military Institute, graduating in the class of 1861. After brief tours as a recruiting officer in North Carolina, and commandant of the camp of instruction at Camp Crabtree in Raleigh; Burgwyn was commissioned as the lieutenant colonel of the newly formed 26th Regiment on August 27, 1861, and later assumed command of that regiment. On July 1, 1863 at Gettysburg, PA, Burgwyn, thought to be the youngest full colonel then serving in the Army of Northern Virginia, commanded the army's largest regiment. The 26th NC, numbering slightly fewer than 900 officers and men advanced toward its epic struggle with the Union's Iron Brigade under the watchful eye of its *Boy Colonel.* In the fierce engagement on the slopes of McPherson's Ridge the 26th NC would suffer the highest losses of any regiment, North or South, during the entire course of the war. At the height of the fighting, with the Colors of the regiment in hand, Colonel Burgwyn was shot through both lungs and mortally wounded. Buried temporarily on the field in an artillery gun case; his body was exhumed through the determined insistence of his mother and returned to North Carolina in 1867, where he now lies buried in Raleigh's Oakwood Cemetery near many of his fallen comrades.

Musician Britton L. Barkley born in 1841, enlisted in the Confederate army at Greenwood, Florida, as a musician. He lost an arm in fighting at Chickamauga, GA, on September 20, 1863, and was sent home. Later, he moved to Raleigh and worked as a night watchman at the state Capitol, living at home on South Blount and South West streets with his wife, a seamstress, and several children. Britton served with Company I of the 4th Florida Infantry. He died in Raleigh in 1890.

Lt. Colonel John Thomas Kennedy of Wayne County was an astute and successful master builder and contractor in the area and through inheritance and business enterprises held vast land holdings. He was instrumental in founding the Wayne Institute and Normal College (1850) and was also a founding trustee of the Wayne Female College that same year. Kennedy also built the first courthouse at Goldsboro and the Bank of New Hanover. In October 1861, Kennedy mustered into State service as a first lieutenant with the 35th North Carolina Troops. Kennedy was appointed to the Field and Staff as assistant regimental commissary in March 1862. In June 1862, he was made captain of Co. B, 62nd Georgia Partisan Rangers. In August 1862, Kennedy was appointed major of the 62nd GA. In July, he was promoted to Lt. Colonel of the 62nd GA cavalry and served with that unit

A Story Behind Every Stone

until the widespread consolidation of the CSA regiments in the spring of 1864. Orders of transfer and consolidation came to Lt. Colonel Kennedy and the 62nd GA and three of its companies (D, E, I) merged with five companies of the 7th Confederate Cavalry Regiment and one company of the 12th NC cavalry battalion to officially make the new 16th Battalion, NC Cavalry. In May 1864, the command was ordered to Petersburg, VA, and all the North Carolina companies were assembled into a new command composed of North Carolina troops. This new unit was designated the 7th NC Cavalry and commanded by Lt. Colonel John T. Kennedy. In June 1864, Kennedy was severely wounded in the back in action near City Point, VA, taken prisoner and held at Bermuda Hundred. He was released by order of Union General B. Butler on August 8, 1864, and sent back to City Point via a flag of truce steamer. The officer returned to Goldsboro on medical leave to recuperate and records indicate that Kennedy was still there in February 1865. John T. Kennedy was paroled on May 5, 1865, at Goldsboro, NC. After the war, Colonel Kennedy became a delegate to the NC Constitutional Convention in 1865; High Sheriff of Wayne County, 1st business manager of the Eastern Hospital for the Insane; a member of the State Senate from Wayne in 1885, and the first assistant curator of the North Carolina Museum in Raleigh.

Private Elkana Aldred of Buncombe County was sixteen years of age when he died in Raleigh on December 13, 1861 of fever. The youngest Confederate Soldier in Oakwood.

Privates Willis G. Hamilton and Wesley G. Hamilton were father and son from Wake County. They enlisted together into Company D, 26th North Carolina Infantry on May 29, 1861. Willis was present in his unit all during the war until paroled at Appomattox Court House, Virginia on April 9, 1865. His son Wesley was wounded at Gettysburg and captured at Burgess'

Mill, Virginia. He was confined at Point Lookout until June 4, 1865. Both father and son entered the Old Soldier's Home in Raleigh together. Willis died in 1895 and son Wesley died 31 years later. Their graves are in sight of each other.

Private Josiah S. Smith of Sampson County, was wounded in the neck and captured at Gettysburg in July, 1863. He was hospitalized at Gettysburg until transferred to David's Island, New York Harbor on July 17. He was paroled to Virginia in September 8, 1863. After returning to duty he was wounded in the leg and jaw and captured at Spotsylvania Court House, Virginia, on May 12, 1864. Josiah died in a Washington, DC, hospital on June 11.

Private Nathan M. Brady was captured at Williamsburg, Virginia, on May 5, 1862, and confined at Fort Monroe, Virginia, until exchanged. He was wounded in the hip and captured at Gettysburg in July 1863. He was hospitalized at Davids Island, New York, until received at City Point, Virginia, on September 16, 1863. Rejoined his company in January 1864, and was present until wounded in the left thigh and captured at Spotsylvania Court House, Virginia, on May 19, 1864. Nathan died in a Washington, D.C hospital of exhaustion from wounds.

Private Joseph A. Miller was born in Germany.

Private Ford Gurney was born in Ireland.

Private Walter S. Henderson was born in Scotland.

Private Thomas Shea resided in Maryland as a tobacconist prior to enlisting in Guilford County, North Carolina, on May 3, 1861. He was discharged about March 2, 1862, "by reason of being a Marylander."

A Story Behind Every Stone

First Lieutenant Frank M. Harney was a carpenter in Buncombe County prior to enlistment. He was wounded at Gettysburg on July 1, 1863, after capturing "with his own hands" the colors of the 68th Michigan or the 150th Pennsylvania Regiment. He died the next day of his wounds.

Corporal Travis W. Singletary was wounded in the summer of 1862, and did not return to his unit until the next year. He was again wounded and captured at Gettysburg. He was hospitalized at Davids Island, New York Harbor, until paroled in August 1863. After returning to duty, he was wounded for the third time in the right leg and captured at Gravel Hill, Virginia. He was hospitalized at various Federal hospitals until he died in a Washington, DC, hospital on January 13, 1865, of chronic diarrhea.

Sergeant William W. Coe was wounded in the right leg and both eyes and captured at Gettysburg. His right leg was amputated and he died in a Federal hospital at Gettysburg on September 17, 1863, of wounds.

Private Jeremiah Huffman of Catawba County was wounded in the hip at Gaines' Mill, Virginia, on June 27, 1862. He was left sick at Gettysburg and captured by the enemy. Jeremiah died on October 20, 1863, in the General Letterman Federal hospital at Gettysburg of febris typhoides. He was the next to the last North Carolina soldier to die at Gettysburg.

Private Robert A. Weeden of Alamance County was wounded in the thigh at Gettysburg on July 3, 1863. "When our color bearer was shot down at Gettysburg he seized the colors and bore them aloft." He died of his wounds on July 23, 1863.

Ensign William M. Chamblee of Nash County was first a private, then a color corporal of Company A of the 47th North Carolina. As color corporal, he was wounded while bearing the flag of his Regiment "in the last charge at Gettysburg." He was wounded at Bristoe Station, Virginia, on October 14, 1863. Again wounded in the fall of 1864, and then promoted to ensign on November 28, 1864, and transferred to the Field and Staff of the 47th. At Hatcher's Run, Virginia, on February 5, 1865, William was wounded in the right thigh. While in the hospital in Richmond, Virginia, he was captured on April 3, 1865. He was hospitalized at Point Lookout, Maryland, transferred to Old Capitol Prison, Washington, DC, transferred to Johnson's Island, Ohio, and was released at Johnson's Island on June 14, 1865, after taking the oath of allegiance.

Privates George W. Smithwich and John W. Smithwich were brothers from Cherokee County, Georgia, and members of Phillips' Legion. They died within three days of each other in the Confederate hospital in Raleigh from febris resmittens.

Private Thomas Byrd of the 53rd North Carolina and **Private Needham T. Byrd** of the 50th North Carolina, were father and son from Johnston County.

Seaman John E. Smith and Private Balthrop Smith were brothers from Granville County. Seaman Smith served on the CSS *North Carolina*, while Private Smith served in the 12th North Carolina. Balthrop was wounded in the shoulder at Gettysburg and captured near Winchester, Virginia. He was confined at Camp Chase, Ohio, until released after taking the oath of allegiance on June 10, 1865.

Private Henry Miller of the Signal Corp of General Hampton's command was a dispatcher bearer for General Robert E. Lee.

A Story Behind Every Stone

Private John A. Melson of Tyrell County was a sea captain before the war and made five trips to China. When the war began, he sold out his interest in vessels and joined the 2nd North Carolina Cavalry.

Private Jacob McGrady of Ashe County was wounded in the side at Fredericksburg, Virginia, on December 13, 1862. At Gettysburg, he was wounded on the third of July in the eye and captured. He died in Union hands eleven days later.

Captain Thomas Norris of Salem, Alabama, served in the 3rd Alabama Cavalry all during the war. He was mortally wounded near Chapel Hill, North Carolina, by the very last shots fired in war from Sherman's Army.

Sergeant Major Francis Robertson of the 1st Arkansas Mounted Rifles is the ranking noncommissioned officer buried in Oakwood.

Private Rufus T. Trexler of Rowan County served in the 46th North Carolina. He was wounded in the foot at Fredericksburg, Virginia, on December 13, 1862; wounded at South Anna Bridge, Virginia, on July 4, 1863; wounded in the foot at Bristoe Station, Virginia, on October 14, 1863; wounded at the Battle of the Wilderness, Virginia, on May 5, 1864; captured at Deep Bottom, Virginia, on July 28, 1864; confined at Point Lookout and Elmira until released on May 29, 1865.

2nd Lieutenant William F. Doles of Nash County served in the 32nd North Carolina. He was captured at Spotsylvania Court House, Virginia, and confined at Fort Delaware, Delaware. He was one of the Immortal 600. These men were sent from the prison camp at Fort Delaware south to Morris Island, on the south side of the mouth of Charleston harbor. They were used as a shield against Confederate artillery fire.

Captain George Mordecai Whiting, a druggist from Wake County, served in the 47th North Carolina. He was wounded and captured at Gettysburg. He was confined at Baltimore, Maryland; Johnson's Island, Ohio; Point Lookout, Maryland and Fort Delaware, Delaware. He "died after the war of disease contracted in prison." George wrote the poem sketched on the west side of the Confederate Monument in the Oakwood Cemetery.

Corporal George W. Stepps of Horry County, South Carolina, served in the 20th North Carolina. He was wounded at Gaines' Mill, Virginia, on June 27, 1862; wounded at Sharpsburg, Maryland, on September 17, 1862; wounded in the groin and captured at Spotsylvania Court House, Virginia, on May 12, 1864. He died in a Federal hospital in Washington, DC, of wounds.

Sergeant William Holt Parsons of the 12th Virginia was a waiter before the war at Whitlock and Grange's Restaurant on East Bank Street in Petersburg, Virginia.

1st Lieutenant Josiah Jones of Wake County was a drill master in the North Carolina Conscript Department.

14 unknown soldiers in one mass grave are probably from Iverson's Brigade and were buried in Iverson's Pit at Gettysburg.

Four Artillery men (all privates), **Neil Marsh** of Company B, **James H. Joyner** and **Alexander Lewis** of Company G of the 2nd North Carolina Artillery, along with **William Perdue** of Company G of the 3rd North Carolina Artillery were all captured at the fall of Fort Fisher on January 15, 1865. They were confined at Elmira, New York, until the sick were paroled and exchanged in late February and early March and sent to the hospital at Richmond, Virginia. Many of their fellow soldiers never made it home (example: 29 members of company G, 2nd NC Arty) and are bur-

Members of the Soldiers' Home band.

ied in Elmira. The four, and others, were soon transferred to the hospital in Raleigh. All three members of the 2nd died on March 20, and Perdue of the 3rd died on April 5. Two are buried in Division one and the other two are buried in Division four. They died of typhoid and pneumonia.

Another artilleryman of Co. A, 3rd NC Artillery, **Private James Carter**, was captured at Fort Fisher on December 25, 1864. He was confined at Point Lookout until exchanged on February 15, 1865, and admitted to Greensboro Hospital on February 21, 1865. He was transferred to the Raleigh hospital where he died on March 8, 1865, of "continuous fever."

The 2nd and 3rd NC Artillery collectively lost 244 men at Elmira and 51 at Point Lookout as prisoners of war. Of the prisoners who were exchanged from the two prison camps, 33 died soon after release and never made it home.

Cemetery Map
Part 1

<<North <<

```
                                    237  236  145  234  144  231  138  228  132
                                         235  146  233  143  230  139  227  133
                                                   232       142       140  226  134
      Division 4              ...                            229  141  225  135
315   217  307                     ...   ...                      E4   224  136
      216         209                                                      137
314   215  306   208  299                           ...   ...
313        305   207  298  200  291
312   214  304   206  297       290        282
311   213  303   205  296  199  289   193  281  185  273  177
310   212  302   204  295  198  288   192  280  184  272  176  265
309   211  301   203  294  197  287   191  279  183  271  175  264  169  258  163
308   210  300   202  293  196  286   190  278  182  270  174  263  168  257  162
           201   292  195  285        189  277  181  269  173  262  167  256  161
      Division 4         194  284     188  276  180  268  172  261  166  255  160
 ...   ...    ...   ...   ...    283   187  275  179  267  171  260  165  254  159
              N3   N4   N5    ...      186  274  178  266  170  259  164  253  158
N1    N2
<     <    << Gen Anderson Monument   ...   ...   ...   ...   ...   ...   ...   ...
                                      ...   ...   ...   ...   ...   ...   ...   ...
 ...          N6        N7        ...
                              ...   ...       81   422   94  107  421  123  140
      Division 8        ...   ...        68   80   423   93  106  637  122  139
                                   55    67   79   424   92  105  636  121  138
435   11   436   32   666   43   54   655   66   78   644   91  104  635  120  137
434   10   21    31   665   42   53   654   65   77   643   90  103  634  119  136
433   9    20    30   664   41   52   653   64             89  102  633  118  135
432   8    19    29   663   40   51   652   63   76   642   88  101  632  117  134
431   7    18    28   662   39   50   651   62   75   641  nw1  100  631  116  133
430   6    17    27   661   38   49   650   61   74   640   87       630  115  132
429   5    16    26   660   37   48   649   60   73   639   86   99  629  114  131
428   4    15    25   659   36   47   648   59   72   638   85   98  628  113  130
427   3    14    24   658   35   46   647   58   71        84   97       112  129
426   2    13    23   657   34   45   646   57   70        83   96  128  111  127
      1    12    22   656   33   44   645   56   69        82   95  nw2  110  126
425  437                                                                 109  125
                 Division 8                                              108  124
```

series 1 = 1861-1865
series 2 = 1870-1909
series 3 = 1909-1938

Path to 'House of Memory' > > >

Archway   ...   .

Series 1 – 1861-1865
Series 2 – 1870-1909
Series 3 – 1909-1938

Next Section

Cemetery Map
Part 2

Division 3

```
223 125 216 117 208 110 199 102 189 ...            Division 3
222 126 215 118 207 111 198     188  92
221 127 214 119 206 112 197 103 187  93 178
220 128 213 120 205     196 104 186  94 177  84   168  75 158
219 129 212 121 204 113 195 105 185  95 176  85   167  76 157
218 130 211 122 203 114 194 106 184  96 175  86   166     156
217 131 210 123 202 115 193 107 183  97 174              155
        209 124 201 116 192 108 182  98 173       165  77 154
                200     191 109 181  99 172  87   164  78 153
                        190     180 100 171  88   163  79 152
...   ...           ...     179 101 170  89   162  80 151
        ...   ...   ...  ...     169      90   161  81 150
                                          91   160  82 149
252 157                                        159  83 148
251 156 247 152                                         147
250 155 246 151 243
249 154 245 150 242 148 240
248 153 244 149 241 147 239 238
```

```
420 nw4 ... 618 166 610 181 601 197 593 213 419  235 250 265
627 nw3 ... 617     609     600 196 592 212 418  234 249 264
626 152 ... 616 165 608 180 599 195 591 211 417  233 248 263
625 151 ... 615 164 607 179 598 194 590 210 416  232 247 262
624 150 ... 614 163 606 178 597 193 589 209 415  231 246 261
623 149 ... 613 162 605 177 596 192 588 208 414  230 245 260
622 148 ... 612 161 604 176 595 191 587 207      229 244 259
621 147 ... 611 160 603 175 594 190     206      228 243 258
620 146 ...             602                  439  227 242 257
619     ...
        145         174     189 586 205 220       226 241 256
        144     159 173 585 188 584 204 219       225 240 255
        143     158 172 582 187 581 203 218       224 239 254
        142 580 157 583 171 578 186 577 202 217   223 238 253
            576 156 579 170 574 185 573 201 216   222 237 252
        141 572 155 575 169 570 184 569 200 215   221 236 251
            568 154 571 168 566 183 565 199 214/555 554 553 552
            564 153 567 167 562 182 561 198    556 557 558 559
                    563

                Division 7

                                            465 464 463
```

Series 1 – 1861-1865
Series 2 – 1870-1909
Series 3 – 1909-1938

Next Section

Cemetery Map
Part 3

```
                                          91   90   89   87   84   80
                                                    88   86   83   79
                             ...                    85   82   78
                                          ....           81   77
 ...   ...                                         ...
 66   146
 67   145  60  135
 68   144  61  134  52  126  48  118      110  ...   ...   ...        ...   ...
 69   143  62  133  53  125  49  117  43  109  38  103   97           ...   ...
 70   142      132  E3  124  50  116  44  108  39  102   96           ...   Conf
 71   141  63  131  55  123  51  115  45  107  40  101   95           ...   Mont
 72   140      130  56  122  54  114  46  106  41  100   94           ...
 73   139  64  129  57  121  E2  113  47  105  42   99   93           ...   ...
 74   138  65  128  58  120      112  E1  104       98   92           ...
      137      127  59  119      111
      136
                         Division 3                ...   ...   ...    ...
                                                                      ...
                                                                      ...
                                                                      ...
 ...  ...  ...  ...  ...  ...  ...  ...  ...  ...  ...   ...   ...    ...   ...
 ...  ...  ...  ...  ...  ...  ...  ...  ...  ...  ...   ...   ...    ...   ...
            Division 7                             ...
 278  294                                          ...                ...
 277  293                         321  335  490                       ...   Flag
 276  292           440  320  334  402         390        378   ...   ...   Pole
 275  291           413  319  333  401         389        377         ...
 274  290           412  318  332  400         388        376   ...   ...
 273  289           411  317  331  399         387        375         ...
 272  288           410  316  330  398         386        374         ...
      287           409  315  329  397  345    385        373         ...
                    408  314  328  396  344    384        372   ...   ...
 271  286  302      407  313  327  395  343    383        371         ...
 270  285  301      406  312  326  394  342    382        370
 269  284  300                          341    381        369
 268  283  299  307 405  311  325  393  339    380        368
 267  282  298  306 404  310  324  392  338    379
 266  281  297  305 403  309  323  391  337              ...
 551  280  296  304      308  322       336                          550
 560  279  295  303                          ...        544  543  542
                                             520  519  518  517  516  515  514
                    ...        505  504  503 502        501  500  499  498  497
      488  487  486 485  484  483     482  481  480  479 478  477  476  475  474
 462  461  460  459 458  457          456  455  454  453 452  451  450  449  448
 ...  ...  ...  ...  ...  ...  ...  ...  ...  ...        HOUSE OF MEMORY      ...
```

Series 1 – 1861-1865
Series 2 – 1870-1909
Series 3 – 1909-1938

Next Section

A Story Behind Every Stone

Cemetery Map
Part 4

```
76  71  66  62  58  54  51  48  ...   SE5  SE3
75  70      61  57  53  50  47  ...   SE6  SE4
74  69  65  60  56  52  49      ...
73  68  64  59  55              ...
72  67  63  ...  ...  Division 2  ...

...  ...  ...  ...  ...  ...  ...  ...              22  SE1  11
     Arlington                                      21   1   10
       Dead                        31  10           20  SE2   9
            Division 1             30  11           19   2    8
...  ...  ...                      29  12           18   3    7
                    25  37  19     28  13           17   4    6
35  46  31  42  26  36  20         27  14           16   5    5
36  45  32  41  27  35  21         26  15           15   6    4
37  44  33  40  28  34  22         25  16           14   7    3
    43  34  39  29  33  23         24  17           13   8    2
        38  30  32  24             23  18           12   9    1
...  ...  ...  ...  ...  ...  ...  ...  ...  ...          SOUTH
...  ...  ...  ...  ...  ...                              GATE
                        S10        Division 5
             ...        S11   350  S7   339  S2   328  ...
     ...        S14  358 S12   349  S8   338  S3   327  ...
                     357 S13   348  S9   S6   S4   S1   ...
         359         356        347       337  S5   326  ...
       S16           355        346       336       325  ...
        Mrs Burgwyn  354        345       335       324  ...
...                  353        344       334       323  ...
S17            S15              343       333       322  ...
...  ...                        342       332       321  ...
     352                        341       331       320  ...
     351                        340                 319  ...
GETTYSBURG                                    330   318  ...
 MONUMENT                                     329   317  ...
                        ...                         316  ...
     Division 6                    ...
549 548 547 546 545
541 540 539 538 537 536 535 534
528 527 526 525 524 523 522 521
513 512 511 510 509 508 507 506            367
496 495 494 493 492 491 490 489       366  363
473 472 471 470 469 468 467 466       365  362
447 446 445 444 443 442 441      438  364  361  360
...  ...  ...  ...  ...  ...  ...   ...  ...  ...  ...
```

Oakwood Ave.

Series 1 – 1861-1865
Series 2 – 1870-1909
Series 3 – 1909-1938

Abbreviations and Explanations of the Alpha List

'D' denotes the eight sections called 'Division' of the Confederate cemetery.

'S' denotes the three different grave numbering systems called series used from year 1877 (when the wooden markers were replaced by stones with numbers) to 1938 (death of the last veteran from the Old Soldiers' Home).

Series 1 numbers 1 to 666 are graves of soldiers that died during the war.

Series 2 numbers 1 to 217 are graves of vets that died from 1890 to October 1909.

Series 3 numbers 1 to 343 are grave of vets that died from September 1909 to 1938.

'G' denotes the grave number assigned to the soldiers, beginning with the first stones placed in 1877 to replace the old rotten wooden markers.

Those without original square markers with numbers:

'Arl' is for the 107 soldiers removed from Arlington Cemetery and reburied in a mass grave in division 1

'N [number]' buried in divisions 7 and 8

'NW [number]' buried in division 8

'E [number]' buried in division 3

'SE [number]' buried in division 1

'S [number]' buried in division 5

'*' before a soldier's names denotes an 'Unknown Soldier' grave stone, but bits of information (possibility incorrect) are noted in the Alpha listings. The hope is that further research can correctly identify these soldiers and they can have a headstone with their name.

Parentheses after the given names designate the place of removal.
   (M) near Mr. Henry Mordecai's land
   (CC) City Cemetery
   (CH) Camp Holmes
   (CM) Camp Mangum
   (WF) Wake Forest
   (Flowlet's fam) location unknown
   (Mrs Price's fam) location unknown
   (Chapel Hill) Chapel Hill

D	S	G	RANK	LAST	GIVEN	CO	NR	UNIT
7	1	560		14 unknowns	—	—	—	NC
1	1	Arl	Pvt	Abernathy	Marion Calvin	H	37	NC
1	1	Arl	Sgt	Adams	George Finley	D	9	NC (1 Cav)
3	2	125	Pvt	Adams	James A.	I	44	NC
3	1	104	Pvt	Adams	James E.	D	50	NC
8	1	421	4thSgt	Adams	James H.			Navy
7	3	248	Pvt	Adams	John F.	B	10	Va Cav
4	1	246	Pvt	Adams	William	I	24	NC
1	1	Arl	Pvt	Adcock	Elvis Green	C	12	NC (2nd co)
6	1	446	Pvt	Aderholt	Jacob E.	D	55	NC
7	1	556	1stSgt	Adkins	William H.	E	53	NC
8	1	424	Pvt	Albritton	Daniel H.	B	4	Fla Inf Batt
3	2	82	Pvt	Alderidge	William R.	C	27	NC
8	3	151	Pvt	Alderman	Henry S.	H	41	NC (3 Cav)
3	1	189	Pvt	Aldred	Elkana C. (CC)	C	29	NC
7	3	282	Music	Aldridge	Bennett Franklin		27	NC Regt Band
8	3	20	Pvt	Aldridge	William	M	22	NC
3	1	135	Pvt	Alexander	Claudius Julius	F	32	NC
7	3	175	Corp	Alexander	James W.	A	11	NC
3	1	165	Pvt	Alexander	Uriah	H	27	Ga Vol Inf
8	3	133	Pvt	Allen	Nathaniel M.	I	6	NC
8	3	118	Pvt	Alley	Andrew Leven	L	21	NC
6	1	458	Pvt	Alley	Isaiah D.	F	47	NC
7	3	186	Pvt	Allison	Norris	H	25	NC
8	3	112	Pvt	Allred	Isaac	G	36	NC (2 Art)
4	1	303	Pvt	Almond	Calvin	H	42	NC
1	1	Arl	2ndSgt	Almond	William J.	F	5	NC
7	3	278	Pvt	Alston	James	A	15	NC Batt Cav
7	1	388	Pvt	Anderson	James A. (M)	I	1	SC Inf (Butler's
4	1	250	1stSgt	Andrew	Samuels S. W.	H	17	NC
8	3	127	Capt	Andrews	George Whitfield	G	50	NC
5	1	333	Pvt	Anthony	David M.	G	43	Ga Vol Inf
8	3	24	Pvt	Apple	Richard Lunsford	E	45	NC
7	1	371	Pvt	Ard	James, Jr.	C	25	SC Inf
6	1	456	3rd Lt	Arent	William R.	H	52	NC
7	1	407	3rdSgt	Arledge	James L.	B	3	SC Batt Reserve
3	1	118	Pvt	Arline	James B.	I	68	NC
8	3	121	Pvt	Armfield	Madison L.	B	72	NC (3 Jr Res)
1	1	Arl	Pvt	Armstrong	Thomas	C	12	NC (2nd co)
1	1	18	Pvt	Arnett	Henry	B	13	NC Batt L Arty
5	3	S10	Pvt	Arthur	Thomas S.	L		SC L. Arty (Ma
3	1	141	Pvt	Ashley	Allen (CC)	C	3	NC Batt L Arty
3	2	112	Pvt	Atkins	William H.	G	13	NC
7	1	373	Pvt	Atkinson	John J.	A	7	SC Batt Inf

A Story Behind Every Stone

BIRTH	DEATH	COUNTY	FATHER	MOTHER	WIFE
	07/../1863				
1834	06/09/1864	Lincoln	Miles B.	Charlotte E. Capps	Jane Wilson Henderson
12/8/1842	04/22/1865	Watauga	Alfred	Elizabeth Flannery	
1843	5/12/05	Pitt	James	Eliza	
1842	06/11/1862	Harnett	Joseph	Telitha	
1840	01/13/1865	Craven			Julia
3/04/1840	3/14/22	Davidson	Henderson	Rebecca Headen	
1826	05/13/1864	Johnston			Martha
1843	05/30/1864	Granville	Henderson	Lucy Edwards	
1830	07/30/1863	Cleveland			Jane
1828	07/02/1863	Surry	James	Lurina V.	
1826	08/10/1864	Taylor	William	Mariah Blackshear	Keziah Slaughter
03/ /1842	5/29/02	Lenoir			
12/ /1841	4/16/16	New Hanover	Owen	Brilliam Benvill	
1845	12/13/1861	Buncombe			
2/17/1843	8/20/25	Lenoir	Howell	Mary	Nancy
1845	12/4/10	Randolph			
1844	05/06/1863	Iredell	Joseph F.	Cecelia Simonton	
0/24/1833	1/14/18	Mecklenburg	J.C.	Catherine	
1841	4/14/1865	Henry	James	Sarah Boynton	
1841	4/30/15	Alamance			
02/ /1830	9/21/14	Stokes	Alfred	Jane	Catharine A. Steel
1841	08/14/1863	Franklin	Francis T.	Beda Alley	
0/18/1838	6/1/18	McDowell	Thomas	Mary Davis	
10/ /1841	6/12/14	Chatham			
2/25/1833	01/23/1865	Stanly	Pleasant	Rebecca Lambert	Darlene Dove
1834	05/24/1864	Stanly	Allen	Isabella	Mary
4/19/1840	5/8/25	Bertie	James	Mary Jane Lawrence	
1845		Anderson	Taylor		
1833	04/08/1865	Martin			
0/25/1837	3/7/15	Rutherford	Samuel	Mira Malinda Groves	
1815	04/07/1865	Jackson			
09/ /1832	4/22/11	Rockingham	Samuel	Eliza Taylor	Jane Murray/Phoeba Sutton
1840	10/20/1864	Williamsburg			
1840	08/06/1863	Lincoln	Jacob	Jane M.	
1818	03/24/1865	Fairfield	Jephtha	Jane	
1844	12/18/1864	Gates	James	Emily	
1847	12/2/14	Cabarrus	Jonathan	Sarah Brown	
1844	05/20/1864	Warren			
	02/02/1865	Cumberland			Caroline (1824)
2/24/1847	5/13/38	Colleton	Thomas S.	Nancy W. Lewis	
1836	03/25/1862	Chowan	Baker	Sarah	Mary
05/ /1836	9/27/04	Edgecombe			
1839	03/13/1865	Kershaw			

D	S	G	RANK	LAST	GIVEN	CO	NR	UNIT
3	2	94	Pvt	Atkinson	Robert M.	A	5	NC
6	1	464	Pvt	Attoway	John Simon	G	1	SC
8	1	426	Pvt	Aubrey	William J.	L	12	La
3	2	E3	Pvt	Ausbon	McGilbray A.	H	17	NC
2	1	88	5thSgt	Austin	James G.	I	53	NC
4	1	294	Pvt	Aydolett	Francis Marion	F	19	NC (2 Cav)
1	2	25	Pvt	Ayers	Joshua Franklin	H	17	NC
1	1	Arl	Pvt	Bailey	Edward L.	A	45	NC
3	1	230	—	* Bailey	T.	B	51	NC
1	2	27	Pvt	Bailey	William H.	H	9	NC (1 Cav)
3	2	45	Pvt	Baird	Thomas A.			NC Home G
4	2	165	Pvt	Baker	Archibald M.	G	51	NC
1	1	23	Pvt	Baker	Evander	B	2	NC Batt Loc
6	1	515	Pvt	Baker	Jessie Johnson	E	20	NC
3	2	67	Pvt	Baldwin	Alfred	C	10	NC (1 Arty)
2	1	83	—	* Baldwin	R. W.		50	NC
1	1	Arl	Pvt	Ballard	Miles M.	E	28	NC
7	1	384	3rdSgt	Ballentine	Jonathan L.	A	6	SC Cav
7	1	398	Pvt	Ballew	James S.	C	1	SC Inf (McC
1	1	Arl	Pvt	Ballington	James N.	C	30	NC
3	2	102	Pvt	Banks	Harrison	A	10	NC (1 Arty)
3	1	179	Pvt	Banks	Tully	B	68	NC
8	3	108	Pvt	Barbee	William H.	E	19	NC (2 Cav)
4	2	217	Pvt	Barden	Samuel James	I	9	NC (1 Cav)
6	1	462	Pvt	Barker	Edward	A	26	NC
1	2	1	Music	Barkley	Britton L.	I	4	Fla
4	1	262	Pvt	Barnes	Jethro	B	50	NC
3	1	124	—	* Barnes	S.	B		NC
3	1	199	Pvt	Barnes	W. A.			NC Conscrip
3	2	145	Pvt	Barrett	William Riley	D	49	NC
8	3	68	Pvt	Bass	Matthew Thomas	C	32	NC
3	1	107	Pvt	Batchelor	William B. (WF)	E	19	NC (2 Cav)
7	3	309	Pvt	Bateman	William C.	K	19	Tenn
3	1	173	.	* Bates	William		17	NC
7	1	387	Pvt	Baughman	John	A	1	SC Arty
3	1	94	Pvt	Baxley	William H.	B	50	NC
4	1	244	Pvt	Baxter	Wallace B.	G	59	NC (4 Cav)
1	1	45	Pvt	Bayles	John J.	G	32	NC
3	2	123	Pvt	Beal	Elija B. H.	H	12	NC
8	3	32	Pvt	Beal	Josiah William	I	23	NC
8	3	34	Pvt	Beam	William S.	I	7	NC
4	1	261	Pvt	Beard	James F.	E	8	NC
3	2	57	Pvt	Beasley	Jasper J.	C	31	NC
7	3	204	Pvt	Beaver	George L.	B	29	NC

A Story Behind Every Stone

BIRTH	DEATH	COUNTY	FATHER	MOTHER	WIFE
1829	2/22/03	Halifax			
1845	08/10/1863	Edgefield		Catharine	
	04/09/1865	Claiborne			
1839	02/02/1899	Martin			
1831	08/06/1862	Union	Bryant E.		Rhoda
1838	02/15/1865	Guilford		Sarah	
1846	04/08/1895	Washington	David F.	Elanor	
1828	07/22/1864	Rockingham	Philips	Jane	Martha A.
	05/15/1864				
1842	01/01/1895	Greene	Elcany	Cherry	
1820	08/07/1897	Person			Lucy R.
02/ /1831	6/14/07	Robeson	Duncan	Sarah Smith	Elizabeth P.
1847	02/03/1865	Cumberland	John	Janet	
1846	07/03/1863	Wayne	Jesse J.	Zilpha Ann	
1821	2/1/01	Lincoln			
	06/19/1862				
1840	07/28/1865	Montgomery	Spencer	Sarah	
1833	03/28/1865	Abbeville			Henrieta
1835	12/21/1864	Richland			
1825	03/13/1864	New Hanover		Mary	
11/ /1831	10/18/03	Edgecombe			
1846	05/10/1864	Currituck		Sarah	
09/25/1844	4/26/14	Wilson	Joseph David	Harriett Dew	
09/ /1832	6/7/09	Duplin			
1841	08/13/1863	Ashe	Levi	Mahola	
10/../1841	02/04/1890	Wake	Benjamin J.	Isabella	M.A.
1842	06/12/1864	Robeson	Phillip		
	02/04/1865				
	02/13/1864				
1831	10/10/06	Moore	Samuel	Elizabeth	
03/ /1828	8/19/12	Northampton	Drewry	Mary Ann Sexton	Mary E. Chambliss
1830	03/22/1865	Nash	James M.	Lucy J.	Aquillo
05/15/1841	9/3/28	McDowell	William	Ellen	
	01/30/1864				
1819	04/07/1865	Abbeville			Margaret
1835	06/12/1862	Robeson	James	Milly	
1845	05/09/1864	Currituck	Thomas E.	Lovey	
1834	11/24/1864	Harnett	Solomon	Nancy	
1836	3/30/05	Nash			
11/ /1827	10/3/11	Granville	Erwin	Lydia	Elizabeth
1845	11/9/11	Iredell	George L.	Rosanna Kerr	
1846	05/20/1864	Cumberland	James S.	Clarissa	
1838	11/30/1899	Wake	Marsh	Ruzilla	Mary E.
02/14/1842	3/9/19	Yancey	Russell	Ruth Anderson	

A Story Behind Every Stone

D	S	G	RANK	LAST	GIVEN	CO	NR	UNIT
1	1	Arl	Pvt	Beck	William	F	13	NC
1	2	SE1	Pvt	Beddingfield	Addison R.	H	31	NC
8	3	90	Pvt	Beddingfield	John P.	F	47	NC
1	2	26	Pvt	Belvin	Nathaniel C.	E	47	NC
3	1	233	Conscr	Bennett	J. T.			NC Conscript
1	2	22	Sgt	Bennett	Joseph E.	B	12	NC
5	1	320	Pvt	Bennett	William F.	D	6	Ga Vol Inf
1	1	Arl	Pvt	Benson	Noah	C	45	NC
3	1	180	Pvt	Benton	Elisha F.	I	68	NC
5	3	S3	Pvt	Biggerstaff	Alfred Webb	F	62	NC
8	3	54	Pvt	Bigham	John Robert	B	25	NC
3	2	61	Sgt	Bingham	George Miller	E	16	NC Batt Cav
1	1	Arl	Pvt	Bird	Robert H.	E	28	NC
7	1	381	Pvt	Black	A. H.	D	1	SC
3	2	106	Pvt	Black	Samuel A.	G	49	NC
3	2	48	Chapl	Black	William Samuel		26	SC
3	1	97	Pvt	Blackley	William J.	C	61	NC
7	3	188	Pvt	Blow	Richard	D	67	NC
3	2	85	Pvt	Blume	William Harvey Sr.	A	52	NC
8	3	120	Pvt	Blythe	James W.	C	37	NC
6	1	520	2nd Lt	Boggan	William W.	H	43	NC
7	1	413	Sgt	Bolling	Edmund P.	K	1	SC Jr Res
5	1	338	Pvt	Bolling	William	H	62	Ga Cav
3	1	196	—	* Boner	J. W.		63	NC
3	2	133	Capt	Boon	Jacob C.	B	7	NC Sen Res
8	3	111	Pvt	Boone	Nichloas	A	30	NC
7	3	263	Pvt	Bowen	James W.	E	35	NC
7	3	320	Pvt	Bowes	James Samuel	A	50	NC
1	1	29	Pvt	Brackens	Adam	I	61	NC
1	1	12	Pvt	Bradley	John (CC)	B	35	NC
1	1	Arl	Pvt	Brady	Nathan M.	A	5	NC
7	3	225	Capt	Brame	Tignal H.		54	NC
7	3	176	Pvt	Branch	Newton A.	D	6	NC
5	1	332	Pvt	Brassell	Titus F.	B	55	Ga Vol Inf
6	1	512	2nd Lt	Bray	William A.	B	2	NC Batt
8	3	36	Pvt	Breedlove	Nathan Harvey	G	43	NC
3	2	111	Pvt	Brewer	Elias A.	A	10	NC Batt H Art
7	3	339	Pvt	Brewer	Wesley D.	L	22	NC
4	1	256	Pvt	Bridgers	Clements	B	15	NC Batt Cav
1	1	Arl	5thSgt	Bridgers	Willie R.	B	2	NC
1	1	Arl	Pvt	Brigman	Anannias	I	53	NC
6	1	475	Pvt	Briley	Tilman T.	K	26	NC
7	3	230	Pvt	Brinson	David H.	B	67	NC
7	1	400	—	* Brise	Y. T.	K	1	SC

A Story Behind Every Stone

BIRTH	DEATH	COUNTY	FATHER	MOTHER	WIFE
1835	07/25/1865	Davidson	Christian	Mary Leonard	Margaret J. Williams
1836	07/15/1887	Wake	Jonathan	Mary	
1830	6/14/13	Franklin			
1823	01/30/1895	Wake			Nancy
	04/08/1864				
1843	09/01/1894	Granville	William M.	Louisa	
1843	05/02/1865	Butts	Benjamin J.	Margaret	
1822	08/07/1864	Guilford			Nancy A.
1844	05/05/1864	Gates		Nancy	
11/16/1843	2/3/23	Rutherford	Samuel P.	Nancy	
08/14/1838	3/30/12	Haywood			
03/30/1824	10/25/1899	Davie	Lemuel	Jane	
1842	05/30/1864	Montgomery	James	Mary	
	02/24/1865				
1824	3/17/04	Cleveland			Martha R.
08/31/1836	08/04/1897	Halifax			Mary Margaret Fleming
1840	01/10/1863	Granville	Thompson	Alethia Hayes	
1845	8/5/18	Wayne			
01/ /1838	6/23/02	Cabarrus	William T.	Unice	
10/25/1839	11/30/14	Mecklenburg	Samuel	Isabella Nantz	
1842	07/02/1863	Anson	James	Sarah	
1847	01/26/1865	Greenville	Thaddeus	Louisa	
	07/08/1864				
04/ /1817	2/2/06	Alamance			M.J.
09/ 1841	6/4/14	Sampson			
1819	6/14/24	Orange			Susan Ann
05/ /1839	11/15/30	Person			
1843	03/13/1865	Alleghany	Joshua	Eliza Louisa	
1837	02/07/1862	McDowell	J.M.	Malinda	
1823	07/08/1864	Guilford			
04/28/1831	7/24/20	Granville	John T.	Elizabeth Smith	
07/14/1833	1/21/18	Burke	Cline	Nancy Coleman	
1846	03/31/1865	Fayette	John C.	Martha C.	
1834	07/01/1863	Surry	Henry C.	Martha	
11/20/1828	11/9/11	Warren	Emauel Harrison	Eleanor Clark	Ann Mariah Clark
1838	9/21/04	Cumberland		Mary	
03/03/1848	5/30/36	Randolph	Andrew	Charlotte White	
1829	06/26/1864	Northampton	Kinchen	Susan	Francis
1842	06/02/1864	Wilson	John	Catherine	
1841	08/08/1864	Union	John	Elizabeth	
1844	09/04/1863	Anson	William K.	Susan	
02/10/1845	10/24/20	Pamlico	Daniel H.	Mary J. Holton	
	03/01/1862				

D	S	G	RANK	LAST	GIVEN	CO	NR	UNIT
3	1	120	—	* Brisson	D.	D	3	NC
4	1	302	Pvt	Britt	Edward (CC)	D	38	NC
4	1	277	Pvt	Britt	Oliver P.	B	50	NC
7	3	284	Pvt	Britt	Richard Thomas	D	59	NC (4 Cav)
5	3	S13	Pvt	Brittain	Isaac James	K	72	NC (3 Jr Res)
3	1	221	—	* Britts	C.			NC
8	3	146	Pvt	Brockwell	Joseph R.	G	28	NC
1	1	Arl	Pvt	Brogden	William G.	C	11	NC
7	1	411	Pvt	Brooks	James	F		SC Holcombe's
8	3	142	Pvt	Brooks	John T.	C	13	NC
8	3	12	Pvt	Brooks	Larkin B.	E	35	NC
1	1	Arl	1sCorp	Broom	Solomon S.	B	43	NC
3	2	103	1stSgt	Brown	Alfred J.	F	40	NC (3 Arty)
3	1	207	Pvt	Brown	Andrew J.			NC Coyette's Ba
3	1	214	Conscr	Brown	D. W.			NC
6	1	513	Sgt	Brown	Jason J.	H	2	NC Batt
1	1	4	Pvt	Brown	John	C	66	NC
1	1	41	Pvt	Brown	Joseph M.	D	71	NC (2 Jr Res)
1	1	Arl	Pvt	Brown	Owen M.	H	8	NC Batt Part.
1	1	Arl	Pvt	Brown	Thomas G.	E	32	NC
1	2	4	Pvt	Brown	William C.	I	47	NC
7	3	319	Pvt	Brown	William R.	C	56	NC
1	2	23	—	* Brown				
7	1	380	2nd Lt	Brownlee	John H.		11	SC Inf
4	1	282	—	* Bryan	A. H.	K	50	NC
6	1	495	Pvt	Bryant	George Andrew	C	43	NC
7	1	418	Pvt	Bryant	John D.	A	44	Tenn
3	2	143	Pvt	Bryant	Joseph John	F	43	NC
6	1	532	Pvt	Bryant	Stephen Nicholas	K	1	NC
2	1	68	Pvt	Bryant	William T.	G	2	NC Arty
8	3	48	Pvt	Buck	Bryan	E	4	NC
1	1	Arl	Pvt	Bullard	James A.	A	46	NC
4	2	149	Pvt	Bunn	George W.	B	47	NC
1	1	Arl	Pvt	Burge	John C. Jr.	F	18	NC
7	3	244	Pvt	Burgess	Hardy B.	F	30	NC
8	3	139	Pvt	Burgess	Isaac Wilborn	A	6	NC
3	1	237	Pvt	Burgess	William T. (CC)	C	3	NC Batt L Arty
5	1	359	Col	Burgwyn	Henry King Jr.		26	NC
5	3	S16	Capt	Burgwyn	Wm Hyslop Sumner	H	35	NC
7	1	405	3rCorp	Burnet	John	I	1	SC (Hagood's)
3	1	140	Pvt	Burnett	William H. (WF)	K	71	NC (2 Jr Res)
4	2	182	Pvt	Burrows	John A.	G	23	NC
4	1	241	Pvt	Butler	Albert T.	C	25	NC
5	1	336	Pvt	Butler	John S.	H	7	Ga Cav

A Story Behind Every Stone

BIRTH	DEATH	COUNTY	FATHER	MOTHER	WIFE
	01/28/1865				
1837	02/26/1862	Sampson	Joel	Penelope	
1845	11/27/1864	Robeson	Elijah	Eliza	
2/03/1844	9/28/25	Hertford	Winston		
3/18/1847	11/20/23	Guilford	John M.	Milliciane	
	03/21/1864				
05/ /1840	2/10/16	Orange	John	Mary Horn	
1845	06/02/1865	Bertie	Henry A.	Millison	
1825	05/19/1864	Abbeville			Tabitha (Roberson)
1844	11/6/15	Caswell			
1829	8/23/10	Person	Matthew	Rebecca	Lizzie J.
1834	07/14/1864	Union	Budy	Nancy 'Beedy'	Elizabeth Hargett
03/ /1839	1/27/04	Wilson			Fanny
	09/07/1863				
	01/05/1864				
1843	07/01/1863	Madison	John	Ruth V.	
1828	03/01/1865	Lenoir			
5/28/1847	03/30/1865	Lincoln			
1824	07/23/1865	Onslow			Ann Hunter
1844	05/31/1864	Catawba		Vina	
1834	01/27/1891	Wake			
4/10/1844	7/27/30	Forsyth	Haywood	Rebecca Lundy	
	11/01/1894				
1839	11/09/1864	Charleston	J.P.	Rebecca	
	12/15/1864				
1826	07/28/1863	Wilson			Priscilla
	08/07/1864				
1838	9/9/06	Halifax	Joseph	Francis	
1829	07/17/1863	Halifax	James S.	Nancy Nichols	Nancy Smith
1822	04/28/1865	Edgecombe			Sarah E.
01/ /1844	2/11/12	Beaufort	Thomas	Levi	
1837	05/29/1864	Robeson	Stephen	Reiney	
08/ /1820	11/7/06	Franklin			Mary
1829	08/01/1864	Rutherford	John C. Sr.	Leah Green	Hester A. Cabines
6/01/1834	12/21/21	Bertie	Jenkins	Eliz. Lassiter	Henrietta
1835	6/20/15	Randolph	John	Louisa Caness	
1846	04/13/1862	Northampton	George	Ann	
9/03/1841	07/01/1863	Wake	Henry King Sr.		Anna Greenough
7/23/1845	1/3/13		Henry King Sr.		Anna Greenough
	04/02/1865				
1847	03/30/1865	Halifax	Jackson	Mary	
1833	2/1/08	Granville			
1845	05/14/1864				
1830	08/12/1865	Bryan			Mary

A Story Behind Every Stone 61

D	S	G	RANK	LAST	GIVEN	CO	NR	UNIT
3	2	77	2nd Lt	Butt	Thaddeus W.	A	8	NC
8	3	110	Pvt	Byrd	Needham T.	D	50	NC
4	1	297	Pvt	Byrd	Thomas	C	53	NC
3	1	119	—	*C	A. A.			NC
7	1	552	Lt	C......	J. A.	G	14	NC
3	1	204	Pvt	Cadle	William	E	13	SC
8	3	117	Pvt	Cain	Struly Howard	D	53	NC
1	1	Arl	Pvt	Cameron	Evander McNair	C	14	NC
6	1	529	Pvt	Campbell	Adolphus L.	C	28	NC
1	1	32	Pvt	Campbell	Daniel	D	46	NC
7	2	346	Pvt	Campbell	Hugh	H	9	NC (1 Cav)
7	3	332	Pvt	Campbell	James M.	B	72	NC (3 Jr Re
8	3	13	Pvt	Canady	A. L.	D	1	NC
8	3	115	Pvt	Cannon	Henry	C	7	NC
3	1	128	Pvt	Capps	John	B	53	NC
1	2	12	Pvt	Carmack	George W.	H	67	NC
8	3	69	Pvt	Carpenter	James L.	D	28	Miss Cav
3	2	49	Sgt	Carpenter	Joshua P.	G	57	NC
1	1	Arl	Pvt	Carpenter	Lemuel	I	43	NC
6	1	490	2nd Lt	Carr	William A.	E	5	NC
3	1	229	Pvt	Carroll	Lewis	F	54	NC
8	3	147	Pvt	Carroll	Thomas Sterling	G	47	NC
3	2	141	Pvt	Carson	James M.	K	2	SC Cav
3	2	131	Pvt	Carter	Francis M.	G	2	NC Batt
4	1	257	Pvt	Carter	James	A	40	NC (3 Arty
8	3	22	Pvt	Carter	James W.	K	12	NC
1	1	Arl	Pvt	Carter	Jesse P.	G	25	NC
8	1	429	Pvt	Carter	John (M)	D	20	Ala
3	2	E2	Pvt	Carter	Omy	I	35	NC
7	1	417	Corp	Carver	R. Elzey	I	9	Va Cav
2	1	61	Pvt	Casper	Justin	C	11	NC
4	1	304	Pvt	Cates	Ephraim	A	50	NC
5	3	S4	Capt	Cathey	George L.	C	Ga Luske	BDE Legion
7	3	180	Corp	Catlett	Augustus A.	F	47	NC
5	1	327	Pvt	Cauley	J. B.	I	7	Ga Vol Inf
6	1	494	Sgt	Causey	Robertson C.	C	45	NC
3	1	228	Pvt	Cauthron	L. Byron	F	9	Va Cav
8	3	91	Pvt	Caveness	James W.	L	22	NC
1	1	Arl	Pvt	Center	Charles H.	H	30	NC
4	2	177	Pvt	Chaffin	Samuel T.	K	8	NC
3	1	145	Pvt	Chamberlain	William	I	42	NC
7	3	158	Ensign	Chamblee	William Melville		47	NC Field &
7	1	554	3rd Lt	Champion	Charles William	G	23	NC
5	1	348	Pvt	Chandler	James Murry	K	6	Ga Vol Inf

A Story Behind Every Stone

BIRTH	DEATH	COUNTY	FATHER	MOTHER	WIFE
04/ /1833	1/4/02	Pasquotank			L.C.
05/ /1842	5/17/14	Johnston	Thomas	Rebecca	
1820	09/28/1864	Johnston	Sutton		Rebecca Sanders
	../../1863				
1826	01/06/1864				
12/ /1835	9/8/14	Bladen	John	Dolly	
1839	01/16/1864	Moore	James R.	Sarah McNair	
1836	07/18/1863	Catawba	John	Elizabeth	
1846	01/16/1865	Robeson	Archibald	Catherine	
02/28/1846	10/14/01				
07/08/1847	9/24/33	Forsyth	Thomas	Emily Fulp	
1830	8/26/10	Guilford			
06/ /1826	7/16/14	Sampson			
1831	01/25/1863	Mecklenburg	John	Nancy	
1845	01/08/1893	Craven	Levi	Penelope	
11/04/1832	8/30/12	Durham			
1831	03/02/1898	Lincoln	Jonas	Sarah	
1822	01/22/1864	Anson			Tempernace
1841	07/01/1863	Greene	Joshua	Nancy	
1845	06/13/1863	Guilford	William	Martha	
06/ /1836	2/23/16	Warren	Sterling	Elizabeth Moore	
1834	9/6/06	Greenville			
1846	12/28/05	Davidson	Giles	Sarah Teague	
1843	03/08/1865	Duplin	Abram	Elizabeth	
1841	2/26/11	Warren			
1844	03/28/1865				
1833	01/03/1865	Bibb			
1821	05/30/1899	Wayne			
1844	07/24/1864	King George	Hiram	Elizabeth	
1842	05/20/1862	Bertie	Henry	Mary	
1821	03/18/1865	Person	Joseph		Nancy
11/27/1822	1/18/23	Macon	William A.	Jennie Lessly	
08/ /1847	4/2/18	Franklin	George	Amanda Cook	
	12/14/1864				
1838	07/21/1863	Guilford	Joseph	Nancy	
	01/02/1865				
1839	6/17/13	Randolph			
1823	05/31/1864	Harnett			
1838	11/16/07	Davie	Archabald H.	Jemima	
1842	08/08/1862	Davidson	Barnabas	Elizabeth	
02/25/1840	8/19/16	Nash	Woodson	Roena Bunn	
1837	07/01/1863	Granville	Charles	Temperance	
7/24/1842	../../1865	Oglethorpe	James Oliver	Emily A. Sims	

A Story Behind Every Stone

63

D	S	G	RANK	LAST	GIVEN	CO	NR	UNIT
7	3	189	2nd Lt	Chandler	William B.	C	13	NC
4	1	298	Pvt	Chapel	H. O.	B	19	NC (2 Cav)
1	1	Arl	Pvt	Chapman	Richard A.	A	6	NC
3	1	202	Sgt	Chappell	Franklin T.	C	26	NC
5	1	346	Pvt	Cheeves	K.	F	34	Ga Vol Inf
4	2	192	Music	Chovey	Benjamin F.	I	5	NC
7	3	316	Pvt	Clagon	Benjamin W.	Ala Montgomery L Art		
8	3	28	Pvt	Clanton	William Drury	B	13	NC
4	1	263	Conscr	Clapp	James R.			NC Mallett's Ba
4	1	255	Pvt	Clark	Noah N.	D	61	NC
1	1	Arl	Pvt	Clark	William L.	H	25	NC
2	1	72	—	* Clarke	M. T.			NC
7	3	310	Pvt	Claytor	Patrick Henry	D	1	NC (6 months
7	3	166	Corp	Claytor	Samuel Baker	E	13	NC Batt L Arty
3	1	226	—	* Cleaveland	W.			NC
8	3	9	Pvt	Clenny	Larry M.	A	23	NC
3	1	95	—	* Clifford	A. J.			NC
7	3	325	Pvt	Cline	Gibson C.	B	20	NC
3	1	164	Pvt	Clippard	John A.	H	52	NC
7	3	262	Pvt	Clopton	Thomas H.	A	44	NC
4	2	152	Pvt	Cobb	Joseph L.	D	40	NC (3 Arty)
6	1	447	Pvt	Cobb	Livingston G.	H	45	NC
6	1	545	Pvt	Cobler	John H.	F	45	NC
7	1	408	—	* Cobrith	J. M.	B		SC
7	3	197	Pvt	Cochran	James W.			Ala Jeff Davis A
6	1	482	Sgt	Coe	William W.	M	21	NC
6	1	367	Col	Colbert	Wallace Bruce		40	Miss
3	1	171	Pvt	Cole	Andrew J.	E	45	NC
1	2	9	Pvt	Coleman	Daniel M.	G	16	NC
4	1	275	Pvt	Coley	John M.	K	28	NC
3	1	110	—	* Collan	H. G.			NC
7	3	276	Pvt	Collins	James M.	F		NC Inf Thomas'Legion
7	3	330	Pvt	Collins	John S.	A	69	NC (7 Cav)
4	2	191	Pvt	Collins	Sumner	E	1	Ala Cav
3	1	109	Pvt	Combs	Nelson	H	17	NC
7	3	324	1stSgt	Commander	Miles	A	8	NC
3	1	136	Pvt	Compton	Lewis R.	I	45	NC
6	1	467	Pvt	Cone	Neverson	A	47	NC
5	1	357	Pvt	Cone	Thomas Jackson	C	55	Ga Vol Inf
3	1	208	Pvt	Conner	L. M.			NC Freeman's Batt PG
3	1	102	—	* Cook	G.			NC
1	1	Arl	Pvt	Cook	Thomas D.	A	10	NC (1 Arty)
7	1	390	Pvt	Cooper	Samuel J. (M)	I	4	SC Cav
4	1	267	Pvt	Cooper	Uriah	A	2	NC Jr Res

A Story Behind Every Stone

BIRTH	DEATH	COUNTY	FATHER	MOTHER	WIFE
01/04/1840	8/5/18	Caswell	Pleasant	Martha Jeffrey	
	02/06/1865				
04/21/1823	04/21/1865	Burke	Joshua	Sarah B. Tallent	Jane
1841	08/29/1863	Wilkes	William A.	Mary	
	03/27/1865	Dade			
08/ /1842	7/5/08	Pasquotank		Rebecca	
07/07/1847	9/22/29	Beaufort			
3/15/1834	6/23/11	Mecklenburg	Drury	Eleanor Beatty	Mary Porter McCorkle
1826	07/27/1864	Guilford			Margaret Reitzel
1844	07/08/1864	Chatham	Hercules	Mary	
1843	04/19/1865	Henderson			
01/24/1838	12/6/28	Orange	Samuel S.	Rachel Cabe	
01/ /1834	12/22/16	Orange	Samuel S.	Rachel Cabe	Elizabeth Lovick
1821	7/21/10	Anson			
04/ /1837	5/22/32	Cabarrus	John	Nellie Joyner	
1842	05/16/1863	Lincoln	Rufus L.	Christina	
03/21/1830	4/19/23	Granville	Ben	Nancy Winston	
1846	1/8/07	Edgecombe	Edward	Mary Belcher	
1827	08/16/1863	Rockingham			
1836	07/06/1863	Rockingham	Thomas	Elizabeth	
	07/30/1864				
03/17/1830	12/16/18	Iredell	William	Sarah Flemning	
1838	09/17/1863	Guilford	John P.	Sybil	
11/17/1834	03/21/1865	Leake	Hines Holt	Martha Ann Beaman	
	03/24/1863	Rockingham			
1831	01/10/1892	Cabarrus			
1846	07/05/1864	Stanly	Samuel	Martha J.	
02/22/1837	10/20/24	Macon	Eli	Lydia Watlen	Catherine
1846	4/3/33	Swain			
04/ /1828	6/21/08	Franklin	Theodorick	Martha Nelms	
1840	05/28/1862	Tyrrell	Spencer		
1845	10/26/31	Pasquotank	Miles	Penelope	
1844	08/18/1864	Caswell	John L.	Nancy	
1843	08/26/1863	Nash	Burkley	Pollie	
1831	03/13/1865	Dooly	Thomas	Frances	Nancy
	01/01/1864				
	02/24/1865				
1836	02/03/1864	Wake			
1844	05/16/1865	Williamsburg			
1/../1847	01/24/1864	Sampson	Sampson	Martha	

D	S	G	RANK	LAST	GIVEN	CO	NR	UNIT
1	1	Arl	Pvt	Coppage	William F.	A	8	NC
3	2	119	1stSgt	Cordon	William W.	K	10	NC (1 Arty)
7	3	255	1sCorp	Couch	William G.	A	66	NC
7	3	252	Pvt	Councilman	William	I	8	NC
8	3	52	Pvt	Cox	Alamander	C	21	NC
8	3	12	Pvt	Cox	Cornelius G.	G	10	SC
1	2	5	Pvt	Cox	John A.	D	49	NC
7	3	280	Pvt	Crabtree	Abram C.	G	14	NC
3	1	137	Pvt	Craig	Harrison	H	42	Ga Vol Inf
6	1	505	Pvt	Crain	Jesse	A	32	NC
7	3	313	Pvt	Cranford	Wilburn M.	F	7	NC
3	1	195	Pvt	Craven	George	F	70	NC (1 Jr Res)
7	1	379	Pvt	Crawford	Virgil	D	3	SC Batt Reserve
7	1	378	Pvt	Crawford	W.		3	SC Batt
1	1	Arl	Pvt	Crawford	William E.	I	5	NC
1	1	Arl	Pvt	Crews	Marcus Aurelius	F	2	SC
8	3	152	Pvt	Crocker	Henry C.	H	47	NC
3	1	132	Pvt	Cross	Barzilla G.	A	56	NC
7	1	392	Pvt	Crosswell	David O. (M)	E	3	SC Batt L. Arty
4	1	285	Pvt	Cunningham	Jesse	D	27	NC
8	3	101	—	Currie	John H.			Navy *Albemarle*
3	1	149	Pvt	Cuthrell	Samuel	K	2	NC
3	1	201	—	* Cutler	George W.		55	NC
4	2	161	Pvt	Dancy	William	E	47	NC
1	1	30	5thSgt	Daniel	Benjamin F.	H	71	NC (2 Jr Res)
6	1	448	Pvt	Danieley	Henry	K	47	NC
8	3	71	Pvt	Daniels	William L.	E	42	NC
6	1	496	—	* Darton	George	C	45	NC
1	1	Arl	Pvt	Davis	Allen M.	E	22	NC
6	1	503	Pvt	Davis	Archibald J.	K	32	NC
7	3	201	Pvt	Davis	Elijah	C	2	NC
1	1	Arl	Pvt	Davis	Hugh W.	K	56	NC
1	1	Arl	Pvt	Davis	James	K	18	NC
2	1	78	Pvt	Davis	Logan C.	A	49	NC
4	2	185	Pvt	Davis	Samuel	C	43	NC
8	3	128	Pvt	Davis	Solomon J.	E	9	NC (1 Cav)
1	1	Arl	Pvt	Davis	William Henry	A	38	NC
7	1	375	Pvt	Dawson	Francis	I	1	SC Inf (Butler's
6	1	486	Pvt	Dearman	William F.	I	16	NC
6	1	471	Pvt	Dees	Clement Allen	B	43	NC
7	1	370	Pvt	Dees	Newitt	C	5	SC Batt Jr Res
8	3	81	Pvt	Delamar	William Bryan	B	67	NC
8	3	18	Pvt	Dellinger	Michael Philip	H	52	NC
8	3	5	Pvt	Dement	Alfonzo J.	B	41	NC (3 Cav)

A Story Behind Every Stone

BIRTH	DEATH	COUNTY	FATHER	MOTHER	WIFE
1844	06/12/1864	Pasquotank	William A.	Sarah Elizabeth	
1840	2/9/05	Beaufort	S.K.	Elen Aim	
7/10/1838	11/4/22	Orange	Thomas	Lila Brown	
1839	6/8/22	Alamance			
04/ /1832	3/20/12	Stokes	Jessee	Polly	
01/ /1847	3/7/15	Horry	Joseph	Cathrine M.	
1835	01/01/1892	Moore	Ivins	Nancy	
5/14/1834	7/6/25	Orange	James	Fannie Hinton	
	09/23/1862	(Walton)			
1840	07/03/1863	Tyrrell	James	Olive	
3/05/1841	1/25/29	Davidson	L.D.	ElizabethRussell	
1847	04/02/1865				
1846	03/26/1865	York	William M.	Martha	
	03/30/1864				
1833	06/17/1864	Randolph			
	10/24/1864		Stanley	Amelia	Isabella
1845	5/1/16	Wake	Jack		
1843	01/04/1863	McDowell			
1845		Sumpter	Gilbert	Lilica A.	
1846	01/20/1865	Lenoir	Henry	Susan	
06/ /1833	2/25/14	Moore			
1839	12/01/1862	Craven			
	01/12/1862				
11/ /1821	5/8/07	Wake			
03/ /1847	03/05/1865	Pitt	Benjamin	Margaret	
1832	08/05/1863	Alamance	Jesse	Nancy	Hettie
1844	9/13/12	Davie			
	../../1863				
2/12/1863	02/12/1863	Guilford	William	Elinor	
1839	07/03/1863	Franklin	James Owen	Sarah	
2/06/1830	1/26/19	Duplin	William	Susan Parker	
1847	04/13/1865	Iredell	Nathan	Margaret	
1842	05/21/1865	Bladen			
1840	05/10/1862	McDowell	John	Obedience	Eliz L.
1817	3/23/08	Wilson			Rachel
3/20/1830	4/8/15	Granville			
1844	08/16/1864	Duplin	Thomas		
1844	04/05/1865	Anderson	Joseph	Frances	
1838	10/13/1863	Henderson	Peter		
1835	09/01/1863	Union	Clement	Elizabeth	
1849	03/24/1865	Chesterfield	Levi	Mary	
1848	2/26/13	Pamlico	William	Ann B.	
09/ /1840	11/7/10	Lincoln	Lewis	Elizabeth Hines	Emily Theodocia Stroup
3/17/1842	1/25/10	Granville	Nelson		Lucissica?

A Story Behind Every Stone

D	S	G	RANK	LAST	GIVEN	CO	NR	UNIT
6	1	546	Pvt	Dempster	John	E	59	NC (4 Cav)
8	3	51	2nd Lt	DeWitt	William L.	I	62	Tenn
5	1	329	Pvt	Dickerson	R. (M)	A	46	Ga Vol Inf
4	2	202	Pvt	Dillard	Jacob	F	52	NC
8	1	422	Gunner	Dillon	Isaiah			Navy *Neuse*
8	3	16	Pvt	Dixon	Jacob	A	24	NC
1	1	Arl	Pvt	Dixon	John U.	I	24	NC
3	2	80	Pvt	Dixon	Sidney L.	K	30	NC
1	1	Arl	Pvt	Dixon	William O.	D	14	NC
6	1	474	Pvt	Dolson	John O.	A	2	US Sharpshoot
4	1	252	Pvt	Dodd	John	D	68	NC
1	1	21	Pvt	Doggett	James G.	I	50	NC
4	2	155	2nd Lt	Doles	William F.	H	32	NC (2nd co)
2	1	84	Pvt	Dowden	Ezekiel	D	50	NC
8	3	138	Pvt	Dowdy	Caleb George	B	3	NC Batt L Arty
1	1	Arl	Pvt	Dowell	Franklin	C	34	NC
1	1	Arl	Pvt	Drake	Francis M.	D	35	NC
8	3	55	Pvt	Drake	Stephen	H	24	NC
5	3	S5	Capt	Drake	William Francis			Va United Arty
3	2	90	Surg'n	Duggan	William A., Dr.			Medical Dept.
8	3	38	Pvt	Duke	Noah H.	E	46	NC
7	3	277	Pvt	Duncan	Abraham D.	D	20	NC
3	2	96	Pvt	Duncan	Gordon Cawthorne	C	12	NC (2nd co)
5	1	316	Lt	Dunnahoo	Thomas Jordan	H		Ga Cobb's Legion Cav
8	3	83	Pvt	Dupree	Robert W.	A	13	NC
1	1	Arl	Pvt	Earby	John	I	5	NC
4	1	292	Pvt	Earls	Joshua B.	D	71	NC (2 Jr Res)
7	3	215	Pvt	Eatmon	Wilson	E	7	NC
3	1	121	Pvt	Edmonds	George (CC)	F	43	NC
3	1	126	Pvt	Edmonson	Andrew McDonnel	B	44	NC
8	3	14	Pvt	Edwards	Alexander C.	K	68	NC
7	3	251	Pvt	Edwards	Alfred L.	F	19	NC (2 Cav)
7	3	165	Pvt	Edwards	John T.	K	63	NC (5 Cav)
4	1	290	Pvt	Edwards	William	A	3	NC Jr Res
7	3	295	Pvt	Edwards	William H.	K	71	NC (2 Jr Res)
1	1	Arl	Pvt	Eidson	William H.	I	5	NC
3	1	146	Pvt	Ellis	Enoch Franklin	H	55	NC
4	2	158	Pvt	Ellis	Jarmon N.	B	56	NC
1	2	17	2nd Lt	Elmore	Charles E.	G	57	NC
8	3	17	Pvt	Elmore	William Phoebe	E	8	NC
7	3	299	Sgt	Elwood	William H.	D	14	NC
8	3	50	Pvt	Emory	Ephraim	A	44	NC
6	1	510	Pvt	Epps	William D.	B	53	NC
6	1	491	Pvt	Estes	Richard B.	H	45	NC

BIRTH	DEATH	COUNTY	FATHER	MOTHER	WIFE
1820	07/04/1863				
02/ /1832	3/18/12	Macon	Prich	Nancy	
	04/27/1865	Upson			
05/ /1824	3/29/09	Wilkes	Thomas	Ruth McBride	Sally Absher
5/06/1864	05/06/1864	Guilford			
05/ /1824	10/11/10	Person			
1838	05/04/1865	Johnston	John	Nancy	
01/ /1823	3/23/02	Mecklenburg			
1841	05/21/1864	Cleveland			
1843	09/03/1863	Minnesota	Charles	Elizabeth	
	06/13/1864				
1834	12/09/1864	Rutherford	George	Elizabeth	
10/ /1825	2/11/07	Nash			Elizabeth
1838	05/30/1862	Johnston	Matthew	Susan	
1839	6/14/15	Currituck	Caleb	Grizzell	
1847	06/30/1864	Alexander	Paton	Easter	Patience
1835	07/12/1864	Chatham			
02/ /1840	4/3/12	Person	William	Elizabeth	
1/14/1839	8/13/30	Northampton	John R.	Martha J. Newsom	Nancy E.
04/ /1841	11/2/02	Edgecombe			Lucy A.
5/24/1834	11/28/11	Granville	Jesse	Nancy	Roann
2/01/1843	3/9/25	Columbus	Abram	Mary Harper	
10/ /1833	3/7/03	Warren	William	Elizabeth	
0/30/1838	04/12/1865	Barrow	James	Jane Jordan	Floreller C. Finch
1842	3/21/13	Caswell			
1833	06/19/1865	Halifax			
1847	02/17/1865	Cleveland	Joshua	Elizabeth	
2/11/1842	2/28/20	Nash	Peter	Minnie Bailey	
1832	03/22/1862	Halifax			
1836	06/02/1862	Martin	Alfred	Lucinda	
1845	8/26/10	Hertford			
5/10/1844	5/13/22	Guilford	Andrew	Ruth Henderson	
5/03/1848	11/3/16	Greene	Isarel	Betsy Macon	Melinda
1847	01/13/1865				
5/17/1846	7/22/26	Warren	William	Sallie Ann Dixon	
1842	05/25/1864	Iredell			
1828	10/28/1862	Alexander	Ben	Mary	Lydia
05/ /1835	4/17/07	Johnston			Esther
1835	01/17/1894	Lincoln			
1834	11/4/10	Cumberland			
1/22/1841	10/12/26	Cleveland	John	Catherine Cook	
05/ /1834	3/16/12	Granville		Fanny	
1832	07/04/1863	York, SC	David Chapman	Miss Lynn	Margaret
1835	07/23/1863	Rockingham			Susan

D	S	G	RANK	LAST	GIVEN	CO	NR	UNIT
7	3	298	Pvt	Ethridge	Amos R., Jr.	NC		Partisan Rangers
1	1	44	—	* Eubank	W.	C	49	NC
8	3	99	Pvt	Eubanks	George W.	D	15	NC
2	1	52	Pvt	Eure	Alfred L.	A	47	NC
3	2	135	Pvt	Eure	Dempsey	B	9	NC (1 Cav)
1	1	Arl	Pvt	Eure	Lafayette L.	B	5	NC
4	2	179	Pvt	Eury	David W.	K	28	NC
7	3	168	Pvt	Evans	George H. W.	E	59	Va
2	1	64	Pvt	Evans	Henry	D	48	NC
4	1	254	Pvt	Evans	John	F	52	NC
3	2	138	Pvt	Evans	Samuel S.	E	23	NC
7	1	404	Pvt	Evans	William S.		2	SC
7	3	326	Pvt	Faggart	Paul A.	A	20	NC
3	2	118	Pvt	Falkner	William Martin	I	24	Miss
1	1	Arl	2nCorp	Fallin	Redmond T.	D	53	NC
3	2	116	Pvt	Farrington	Loton W.	E	2	NC
7	3	187	Pvt	Farrior	George F.	A	71	NC (2 Jr Res)
8	3	40	Pvt	Felton	Ivey Wooten	E	19	NC (2 Cav)
8	3	47	1stSgt	Ferguson	George P.	B	1	SC Cav
4	1	240	Pvt	Ferolic	James H.	H	70	NC (1 Jr Res)
8	3	39	Pvt	Ferrell	Thomas Jefferson	C	47	NC
1	1	27	Pvt	Fields	Doctor G.	K	20	NC
7	3	268	Pvt	Finch	Henry Bunn	A	10	NC (1 Arty)
7	3	253	Pvt	Finch	William S.	G	23	NC
7	3	257	Pvt	Finger	Daniel	A	12	NC
2	1	60	Pvt	Fish	William Henry	F	32	NC
3	1	234	—	* Fisher	P. F.	I	1	NC
1	1	40	Pvt	Flake	John R.	I	67	NC
7	1	389	4thSgt	Fleming	Thomas B. (M)	I	4	SC Cav
8	3	46	Pvt	Fletcher	Matthew	F	13	NC
6	1	548	Corp	Flowers	W. H.	C	59	NC (4 Cav)
8	1	428	Capt	Floyd	John B. (Mrs. Price's Farm)		9	Ala Cav
3	2	100	Pvt	Ford	Henry W. P.	B	44	NC
4	2	159	Corp	Forney	Sidney J.	H	52	NC
6	1	479	Corp	Forrest	Samuel P.	K	28	NC
1	1	Arl	Pvt	Forshee	William T.	I	14	NC
1	1	Arl	Pvt	Foust	John, Jr.	E	10	NC (1 Arty)
7	3	247	Pvt	Fowler	James W.	E	8	NC Batt
8	3	29	Pvt	Fowler	John W.	A	5	NC
1	1	33	Pvt	Fowler	Joseph S.	B	10	NC (1 Arty)
7	3	236	Pvt	Fox	Cain	G	37	NC
3	2	128	Pvt	Fox	William A.	F	29	NC
4	2	166	Pvt	Foy	Morris	B	24	NC
8	3	10	Pvt	Francis	Samuel	K	1	NC

A Story Behind Every Stone

BIRTH	DEATH	COUNTY	FATHER	MOTHER	WIFE
10/06/1845	10/6/26	Dare	Amos R.	Louise H. Paugh	
	05/27/1862				
09/ /1833	2/22/14	Chatham			
1842	05/28/1862	Nash	Alfred	Jincy	
08/ /1811	5/19/06	Gates			Elizabeth
1841	04/13/1865	Gates			
11/ /1836	11/3/07	Stanly	Abram	Nancy	
12/01/1835	2/5/17	Caswell	George	Mary Langhius	
1832	05/12/1862	Moore			Effie (1820)
1836	06/25/1864	Wilkes	Jesse	Nancy	
05/ /1830	7/1/06	Granville	Thomas	Fanny	
	03/01/1865				
07/15/1843	6/22/32	Cabarrus	Soloman	Sophia House	
1837	2/4/05	Mecklenburg			
1831	04/12/1865	Stokes	William	Elizabeth	Bettie
1834	1/8/05	Guilford	Nathaniel	Patsy	Martha J.
01/04/1847	6/1/18	Duplin	John	Elizabeth	
1843	12/10/11	Wilson	John	Tanzy	
1829	2/6/12	Laurens			
	../../1865				
11/ /1834	12/8/11	Wake	William	Mary	Rebecca
1834	03/18/1865	Columbus	Curtis	Mary	M.
02/12/1843	1/20/24	Wake	William	Sophrinia Haynes	
06/01/1834	9/20/22	Granville	William	Bessie Hutchpeth	
06/24/1842	12/5/22	Catawba	James	Elizabeth	
1838	08/17/1862	Catawba	John	Susan	
	12/01/1862				
1847	03/03/1865	Pitt	Samuel	Piscilla	
1836	05/01/1865	Williamsburg	Edward P.	Elizabeth M.	
11/ /1842	2/4/12	Ashe			
	07/04/1863	New Hanover			
	04/14/1865				
11/ /1845	6/6/03	Edgecombe			
09/ /1843	4/17/07	Lincoln	Capt. A.E.		
1842	09/17/1863	Stanly	William	Mary	
1839	06/17/1864	Davidson	Ira	Emeline	
1827	07/25/1865	Rowan			
08/ /1834	1/29/22	Orange	Samuel	Jennie Collins	
04/23/1836	8/7/11	Cumberland			
1839	03/30/1865	Craven	Joseph	Mary Ann	
12/09/1843	3/29/21	Alexander	Hugh	Sarah Shook	Luisa Drum
1833	7/28/05	Yancey			Elizabeth
1834	6/17/07	Onslow			Mary Fisher
1842	7/22/10	Halifax			

A Story Behind Every Stone

D	S	G	RANK	LAST	GIVEN	CO	NR	UNIT
7	3	304	Pvt	Franklin	John H.	E	14	NC Batt Cav
3	1	122	—	* Frazier	George (WF)			NC
1	1	Arl	Pvt	Frazier	Joshua D.	F	37	NC
6	1	465	Pvt	Freeman	John C.	E	6	NC
2	1	90	Pvt	Freeman	Terrell W. (CC)	G	35	NC
4	2	150	Pvt	Freeman	William James	D	27	NC
7	3	241	Pvt	Freeze	S. Andrew	E	49	NC
3	2	65	Sgt	Friddle	Eli	L	21	NC
3	1	192	Pvt	Fry	L. P.	D	27	NC
4	1	265	Pvt	Fulk	Augustine	F	21	NC
7	3	222	Pvt	Fuller	Henry F.	D	2	NC
2	1	76	Pvt	Furr	Abraham	F	26	NC
2	1	59	Pvt	Gaddy	Stephen T.	K	43	NC
3	1	108	Pvt	Gardner	James Lafayette	G	49	NC
7	3	249	Pvt	Gardner	William G.	B	26	NC Batt
3	1	114	—	* Garrett	W.		14	NC
5	3	S6	Music	Gates	Dudley H.		19	NC (2 Cav) Bar
3	2	87	Pvt	Gavin	William A.	B	51	NC
6	1	502	Pvt	Gay	Gilbert G.	F	43	NC
3	2	69	Pvt	Gay	Solomon	E	38	NC
6	1	441	Pvt	Geringer	John H.	H	1	NC
1	1	Arl	Pvt	German	James C.	D	9	NC (1 Cav)
6	1	521	Pvt	Gilbert	James M.	E	52	Va
1	2	8	Pvt	Gilbert	Martin Van Buren	L	17	NC
6	1	443	Pvt	Gilbert	William	D	23	NC
8	3	113	Lands	Gill	Ezra Thomas			Navy *Yadkin*
1	1	Arl	Pvt	Gillespie	James H.	H	2	NC Batt
4	1	296	Pvt	Gilliam	John	A	9	NC (1 Cav)
6	1	487	Pvt	Glasscow	Andrew Jackson	H	21	NC
7	1	559	Pvt	Glen	Hinton Coslett	C	6	NC
2	1	50	Pvt	Godfrey	Richmond	G	44	NC
7	3	170	Pvt	Godsey	William Henry	B	56	Va
4	2	164	Pvt	Goins	William Daniel	I	19	NC (2 Cav)
7	3	338	Pvt	Gooch	William Lee	K	14	NC
2	2	SE6	Capt	Goodloe	Lewis D.	I	35	NC
5	1	319	2nCorp	Goodwin	Ebenezer J. (M)	E		Ga Bonaud's Ba
3	2	59	Pvt	Goodwin	George L.	C	47	NC
2	1	67	Pvt	Gotier	John C.			NC Conscript
3	1	139	Sgt	Gracie	John G.	I	6	NC
2	1	81	Pvt	Grant	James (CM)	G	56	NC
4	2	170	3rd Lt	Gray	Timothy Iredell	H	17	NC (2nd co)
6	1	452	Pvt	Green	Drury A.	D	55	NC
7	1	377	Pvt	Green	James M.	E	1	SC Arty
7	3	272	Pvt	Green	William R.	I	55	NC

A Story Behind Every Stone

BIRTH	DEATH	COUNTY	FATHER	MOTHER	WIFE
5/24/1844	7/6/27	Haywood	Eason	Margaret England	
1847	07/07/1864	(Yancey)			
1840	08/21/1863	Alamance			
1841	01/10/1862	Henderson			
07/ /1829	12/13/06	Lenoir			
1844	9/14/21	Iredell	William	Hannah	Elizabeth
05/ /1817	10/10/00	Orange			
	01/25/1864				
1836	06/12/1864	(Stokes)			
4/15/1832	5/30/20	Nash	Samuel	Sallie Taylor	
1846	08/16/1862	Caldwell			
1837	02/01/1864	Anson	Clement	Sarah	
1816	07/31/1862	Cleveland	Thomas	MaryOlive Martin	Ann Elvira Cornwell
4/12/1846	3/16/22	Rowan	John	Nancy Coon	
1/22/1836	4/8/25	Orange		Elizabeth	
12/ /1845	8/27/02	Duplin	Samuel L.	Adaline	
1839	07/01/1863	Halifax		Nancy Hancock	
03/ /1832	6/1/01	Richmond	John	Lydia	Dorathia
1839	07/28/1863	Alamance	Jesse	Levina	
1845	04/07/1865	Caldwell			
1845	07/05/1863				
1836	09/02/1888	Wake			
1834	08/15/1863	Caldwell	John	Ann	
08/ /1841	6/22/14	Franklin	Ezra	Alice Davis	
1842	08/16/1864	Madison			
1835	09/19/1864	Wilkes	James	Sylvia	
1839	10/18/1863	Surry			
1842	07/04/1863	Orange	Duncan C.	Serey	
1831	06/02/1862	Alamance	John	Nancy	Sylva
3/10/1836	3/16/17	Mecklenburg	William	Mary Freeman	
11/ /1823	6/7/07	Moore			
/01/1838	2/9/36	Wake	Tom	Nancy Good	
1839	09/08/1883	Warren	Henry	Indiana L.	
1823		Monroe			
1824	12/31/1899	Wake			Nancy
1836	08/14/1862	Sampson			
	12/17/1862	Wake			
1835	07/17/1862	Henderson	Andrew	Sarah Decker	Elizabeth Hollingsworth
06/ /1844	7/8/07	Pitt	Timothy McC		Martha I.
/29/1836	08/20/1863	Rutherford	John	Aletha McKinney	Elizabeth Bridges
1843	03/26/1865	Sumpter	John L.	Lattie D.	
1846	8/9/24	Vance	Nathan	Alica Thomas	

A Story Behind Every Stone

D	S	G	RANK	LAST	GIVEN	CO	NR	UNIT
1	1	Arl	Pvt	Greenway	Samuel	G	30	NC
1	1	Arl	Pvt	Griffin	Claudius P.	D	6	NC
7	1	410	Pvt	Griffin	Stephen H.	F	4	SC Cav
1	1	Arl	Pvt	Griffin	Zachariah H.	E	45	NC
7	1	551	3rd Lt	Griffith	James A.	G	14	NC
7	3	337	Pvt	Grimes	Jacob T.	C	13	NC Batt L A
8	3	7	Pvt	Groce	William H.	D	35	NC
7	1	414	Pvt	Gunnell	James G.	H	24	Va
3	2	70	Pvt	Gurganious	George F.	A	41	NC (3 Cav)
4	1	260	Pvt	Gurley	James Frank	F	71	NC (2 Jr Res
2	1	55	Pvt	Gurney	Ford	H	12	NC
1	1	35	Corp	Guy	Lewis H.	I	51	NC
3	1	168	Maj	*H.	L. M.			NC
4	2	172	Pvt	Hackney	Thomas L.	K	1	NC
1	1	Arl	—	*Hadley	Franklin	D	28	NC
7	3	297	Pvt	Hadley	William Blount	F	17	NC
6	1	481	Pvt	Hager	Sidney H.	K	23	NC
3	1	206	Pvt	Hagler	Darling M.	I	48	NC
1	1	Arl	Pvt	Hagler	Hiram	H	30	NC
7	3	237	Pvt	Hair	James D.	I	46	NC
2	1	89	Pvt	Hall	Andrew J.	E	53	NC
1	1	Arl	Pvt	Hall	Harrison	E	53	NC
8	3	76	Pvt	Hall	John W.	E	28	NC
5	1	345	2nd Lt	Hamilton	Matthew Thompson	F	19	Ga Vol Inf
6	1	504	Pvt	Hamilton	Miles R.	E	32	NC
7	3	289	Pvt	Hamilton	Wesley G.	D	26	NC
1	2	35	Pvt	Hamilton	Willis Gaston	D	26	NC
3	1	193	Conscr	Hamlett	H.			NC
7	1	395	Pvt	Hammett	R. K. B.	E	27	SC
3	2	130	Music	Hampton	Wiley P.		46	NC Regt Ba
1	1	Arl	3rCorp	Hamrick	Asa	H	28	NC
7	1	558	Pvt	Hancock	John A.	D	52	NC
3	2	74	Pvt	Hancock	John R.	D	1	NC
1	2	20	Pvt	Hand	Owen	G	19	NC (2 Cav)
3	2	124	Pvt	Harden	George L.	G	41	NC (3 Cav)
5	3	S1	Pvt	Harden	William Henry	C	16	NC Batt Cav
8	3	132	Pvt	Hardin	Zachariah C.	G	16	NC
1	1	Arl	Pvt	Hardy	Francis M.	B	30	NC
4	1	288	Pvt	Hardy	J. H.	H	71	NC (2 Jr Re
3	2	99	Pvt	Hardy	James R.	B	13	NC Batt L A
3	2	132	Pvt	Harkey	David Monroe	F	9	NC (1 Cav)
1	1	1	Sgt	Harlow	William Shepard	D	3	NC
7	3	194	Pvt	Harman	Henry Holmes	H	37	NC
6	1	525	1st Lt	Harney	Frank M.	F	14	NC

A Story Behind Every Stone

BIRTH	DEATH	COUNTY	FATHER	MOTHER	WIFE
1822	12/31/1863	Granville			
1845	07/10/1864	Union	Thomas B.	Jane	
	07/30/1864	Colleton			
1840	04/16/1865	Rockingham	William	Mary	
1841	07/01/1863	Rockingham	A.A.	Jane R.	
04/09/1845	6/9/35	Davidson	Jacob T.		
1839	4/12/10	Yadkin	Henry	Sarah	
1821	04/17/1863	Patrick			Jane
08/ /1827	7/21/01	Greene			
1848	12/12/1864	Union	John	Sarah Ellen	
1829	02/22/1864	Halifax			
1835	03/25/1865	Cumberland	James		
04/ /1833	7/13/07	Halifax			Martha Edwards
11/13/1845	9/11/26	Martin	Thomas B.	Frances Smithwick	Sarah E.
1843	09/18/1863	Mecklenburg		Sarah	
1830	02/01/1863	Union			Elizabeth C.
1821	08/03/1864	Union	Peter	Margaret Polk	Rosanna Rushing
1841	4/14/21	Sampson	Tom	Bedie Howard	
1838	06/15/1862	Surry			
1842	07/27/1864	Surry	Isaac	Sarah	
06/ /1836	1/1/13	Montgomery	Henry B.	Willa	
1838	03/21/1865	Carroll	John Lewis	Margaret I. Reid	
1834	07/02/1863	Catawba	Dury	Mary	
12/02/1843	1/25/26	Wake	Willis G.	Margarett Beamer	
1822	12/15/1895	Wake			Margarett Beamer
	04/10/1864				
	01/29/1865				
1830	9/19/05	Granville	Zachary	Sally	
1840	06/13/1864	Cleveland			
1843	07/01/1863	Yadkin	Andrew	Nancy	
11/ /1825	10/8/01	Orange			
1821	06/23/1894	Beaufort			
1839	4/21/05	Halifax	Henry		
08/13/1843	11/2/25	Greene			
03/ /1843	4/28/15	Rutherford	William	Artelecia	
1842	08/17/1864	Warren			
	03/02/1865				
1834	5/17/03	Martin			
08/29/1826	1/17/06	Cabarrus	David	Catherine Eudy	Margaret Smith
1818	02/20/1865	New Hanover			
1838	11/14/18	Gaston	Henry	Sallie Collier	
1838	07/02/1863	Buncombe			

A Story Behind Every Stone

D	S	G	RANK	LAST	GIVEN		CO	NR	UNIT
3	2	115	Pvt	Harper	Allen		D	10	NC (1 Arty)
1	1	Arl	Pvt	Harrell	John A.		I	53	NC
3	2	43	—	* Harris	J. S.				
3	2	101	Pvt	Harris	Jesse T.		I	47	NC
1	2	21	Pvt	Harris	John C.		H	11	NC
8	3	126	Pvt	Harris	Ridley L.		B	13	NC Battery
6	1	530	Pvt	Harris	Samuel		F	45	NC
2	1	73	Pvt	Harris	William D.		G	47	NC
7	3	275	Pvt	Harrison	Walter N.		G	70	NC (1 Jr Res)
3	1	129	Sgt	Harrison	William J.		D	17	NC (2nd co)
8	3	89	Pvt	Hartgrave	Joseph F.		I	62	NC
1	1	17	Pvt	Hartsell	Jonah A.		H	42	NC
5	1	330	Pvt	Hartsfield	Robert F.	(M)	K	6	Ga Vol Inf
1	2	11	Pvt	Hasten	William		K	48	NC
4	2	195	Pvt	Hatch	James R.		G	67	NC
3	2	72	Pvt	Hathcock	Jessie John		H	14	NC
3	2	137	Pvt	Hawkins	Dallas		F	1	Missouri Cav
1	1	43	Pvt	Hays	Calvin		F	58	NC
4	1	247	Pvt	Hays	John		K	68	NC
8	3	26	Pvt	Haythcock	William H.		D	44	Va
3	2	53	Pvt	Hazard	Samuel		D	27	NC
7	3	274	Pvt	Heard	John		C	10	Va Cav
3	2	136	Pvt	Heath	James P.		A	3	NC
7	3	159	Pvt	Heath	James Washington		I	22	NC
8	3	NW3	Pvt	Heavlin	Robert A.		E	9	NC (1 Cav)
8	3	66	Pvt	Hedgepeth	Alford D.		A	11	NC
4	1	309	Pvt	Hedrick	William F.		C	70	NC (1 Jr Res)
3	1	224	Pvt	Heffler	R. H.				NC McRae's Batt Cav
7	3	203	Pvt	Hefner	Sylvanus		A	25	NC
1	1	8	—	* Hegewert	J.				NC
2	1	58	Pvt	Helms	Joshua		A	48	NC
1	1	46	Pvt	Helton	Jacob		C	70	NC (1 Jr Res)
8	3	150	Pvt	Henderson	James A.		B	6	NC
1	1	9	Pvt	Henderson	John		H	67	NC
3	2	40	Pvt	Henderson	Walter S.		K	15	NC
7	3	209	Pvt	Henkle	William O.		K	4	SC
4	2	154	Pvt	Henry	Harvey M.		E	29	NC
7	3	196	Pvt	Henry	William L.		E	69	NC (7 Cav)
7	3	226	Pvt	Herbert	William T.		K	71	NC (2 Jr Res)
5	1	350	Pvt	Herring	R. S.		I	1	Ga Vol Inf
7	1	409	Pvt	Herrington	John Kinder		I	25	SC Inf
1	1	Arl	Pvt	Hicks	Joseph		D	56	NC
1	1	20	Pvt	Hicks	R. N.		D	2	NC Batt Jr F
8	3	137	Pvt	Hicks	William H.		D	31	NC

A Story Behind Every Stone

BIRTH	DEATH	COUNTY	FATHER	MOTHER	WIFE
05/ /1840	12/24/04	Edgecombe			
1829	08/07/1864	Union		Elizabeth	Jane
	05/12/1896				
09/ /1830	7/7/03	Wake			
1829	09/21/1894	Mecklenburg			
01/ /1848	3/6/15	Warren			
1834	07/15/1863	Rockingham	Charles W.	Cyntha	
1812	06/03/1862	Nash			
1848	9/19/24	Caswell	Caloway J.	Prudence H.	
1828	04/02/1865	Martin	Davis B.	Wincy	Drewsiley
1845	5/31/13	Haywood	A.C.	Ellinder	
1838	01/31/1865	Stanly	James L.	Elizabeth	
4/1/1846	05/22/1865	Oglethorpe	Berry	Martha Glenn	
1819	11/30/1892	Forsyth	William	Elizabeth	
1845	10/19/08	Lenoir	E.H.	Louiza M.	
1832	8/13/01	Stanly	James	Mary	Sarah Hinson
01/06/1836	6/2/06	Halifax	Reddin J.	Eliza Pierce	Cora Carrington
	03/28/1865	Burke			
1830	05/09/1864	Northampton			Eliza M.
1843	5/18/11	Halifax			
1824	11/06/1898	Lenoir			Harriett
04/18/1841	9/12/24	Wake	William	Mary Merddigh	
12/ /1834	5/27/06	Greene			
07/10/1837	8/28/16	Guilford	Erwin	Sally Webb	
01/ /1836	5/31/16	Granville	John	Lethe Kimble	
12/ /1840	7/29/12	Wilkes			
1847	03/30/1865	Davidson	Valentine	Elizabeth	
	04/05/1864				
01/23/1842	2/21/19	Catawba	Daniel	Barbee Baker	
	03/25/1865				
05/11/1831	08/30/1862	Union	Emanuel	Mary Pyron	Caroline Catherine Crowell
1847	04/18/1865	Davidson	Joseph	Patience	
06/ /1841	4/13/16	Orange	Adolphus	Betsey Parker	
	03/ /1865	Duplin			
1815	04/24/1896	Edgecombe			Elizabeth Bradley
04/05/1839	10/17/19	York	Jacob	Jane Adkins	
1846	1/19/07	Haywood		Avaline	
02/28/1846	12/13/18	Haywood	Lorenzo M.	Mary Moore	
05/10/1846	8/8/20	Halifax	Abner	Elizabeth Smith	
	09/29/1864				
1847	07/18/1864	Clarendon	Joseph Zachariah		Elizabeth Kinder
1838	04/15/1865	Orange			
1847	11/25/1864				
01/12/1840	5/27/15	Wake	William	Cornelia Hayes	

D	S	G	RANK	LAST	GIVEN	CO	NR	UNIT
4	2	151	Pvt	Hicks	William M.	E	26	NC
8	3	148	Pvt	Hight	Jordan S.	E	47	NC
1	1	Arl	Pvt	Hildreth	James	I	43	NC
1	1	Arl	Pvt	Hill	James E.	D	18	NC
3	1	131	Pvt	Hill	Jonathan	D	43	NC
4	1	251	Pvt	Hill	Richard Ausker	I	24	NC
8	3	93	Pvt	Hill	William Lemuel	K	67	NC
4	2	190	Capt	Hines	James M.	K	45	NC
7	3	156	Pvt	Hines	Joel	I	10	NC (1 Arty)
5	1	358	Sgt	Hodges	Wiley Franklin	D	66	Ga Vol Inf
1	2	16	Adj	Hoey	John E.		29	NC Staff Adjuta■
7	3	343	Pvt	Holcomb	William T.	I	28	NC
3	2	68	Pvt	Holden	Sylvanus	C	13	NC Batt L Arty
1	1	3	Pvt	Holder	Thomas	H	72	NC (3 Jr Res)
7	3	198	Sgt	Holderby	John M.	H	45	NC
7	3	292	Pvt	Holeshouser	Crawford	K	4	NC
1	1	Arl	Pvt	Holland	William	I	6	NC
4	1	313	Pvt	Hollis	Edward	E	17	NC
3	1	184	Pvt	Holloway	Martin (CC)	A	34	NC
7	3	296	Pvt	Holloway	Nathaniel Woodard	I	70	NC (1 Jr Res)
1	1	10	Corp	Honeycutt	James Adams	H	42	NC
3	2	126	Pvt	Hooper	Allen J.	C	41	NC (3 Cav)
1	1	Arl	—	*Hoosing	Jas. D.		42	NC
2	1	71	Pvt	Hoots	William	F	52	NC
7	3	233	Sgt	Hopkins	Barney H.	H	38	NC
4	2	199	Pvt	Hopkins	David Allen	H	31	NC
2	1	70	Pvt	Hopkins	James Franklin	G	17	NC (2nd co)
8	3	65	Pvt	Hopper	Adolphus Winfield	F	1	Engineer Troop
7	3	162	Pvt	Hoppes	Jonathan H.	B	54	NC
3	1	219	Pvt	Hornback	Eli	E		NC Mallett's Ba
1	1	Arl	Pvt	Horne	Sidney A.	C	53	NC
6	1	450	Pvt	Horne	William B.	H	43	NC
4	1	281	Pvt	Horton	Hollis J.	F	71	NC (2 Jr Res)
8	1	433	2nCorp	Horton	James Wiley	B	40	Ala
1	1	Arl	Pvt	Horton	William Henry	A	5	NC
4	2	167	Pvt	House	James			NC Home Gua■
3	2	93	Pvt	Howard	Henderson O.	E	10	NC (1 Arty)
7	3	264	Pvt	Howard	Samuel M.	K	65	NC (6 Cav)
8	3	73	Pvt	Howland	Samuel L.	G	10	NC (1 Arty)
7	3	266	Pvt	Hoyle	James R.	H	9	NC (1 Cav)
4	2	162	Pvt	Hoyt	James H.	K	3	Ala
8	3	75	Pvt	Hubbard	George Dallas	F	13	NC Batt L Arty
5	1	356	Pvt	Hudgins	R. B.	D	27	Ga Vol Inf
3	1	151	Pvt	Hudson	Aquilla	H	2	NC Batt

A Story Behind Every Stone

BIRTH	DEATH	COUNTY	FATHER	MOTHER	WIFE
1839	12/14/06	Chatham			
)9/ /1844	2/25/16	Wake	Bennett	Malassi Duke	
1835	01/21/1864	Anson			
1841	05/31/1864				
1832	08/14/1863	Rutherford	Charles	Francis Blankenship	Jane
1833	../../1865	Wake	Wiley	Kiddy Hartsfield	Susan Barbee
1844	7/21/13	Wayne	John	Nancy	
1837	6/18/08	Pitt	Peter E.		
3/12/1845	8/10/16	New Hanover	Isaac	Kate Register	
1822	03/13/1865	Washington	Jordan	Mary Miller	Margaret Jane Smith
1835	11/09/1893	Cleveland			
3/15/1840	5/22/38	Yadkin	George L.	Nancy Chappell	
)8/ /1843	5/3/01	New Hanover	William	Betsy	
1846	02/22/1865	Cumberland	George	Nancy	
)/15/1843	12/28/18	Rockingham	George Hiram		Delila Moorehead
)5/ /1841	4/6/26	Rowan			
1828	08/04/1864	Randolph			Nancy C.
1814	03/28/1865	Martin			
1836	02/20/1862	Ashe	Isaac	Polly	
)/07/1846	8/5/26	Wake	Nathaniel	Nancy Woodard	
1846	02/22/1865	Stanly	Lewis	Mary	
1839	6/14/05	Caswell			
1838	06/06/1862	Wilkes	Jacob	Nancy	
!/30/1840	2/23/21	Randolph	Martin	Elizabeth Stide	
)1/ /1837	11/24/08	Wake	Richard Jackson		Mary E. Pugh
1844	08/19/1862	Washington	Jordan	Louisa	
1847	7/19/12	Rockingham	Samuel S.	Julia	
)6/ /1840	10/26/16	McDowell			
1846	01/06/1864	Union	Dean L.		
1844	07/15/1865	Johnston	Benjamin	Elizabeth	
1/2/1829	08/18/1863	Anson	William	Martha Boggan	Sara M. Preslar
1847	12/09/1864	Union	Bartlet	Elizabeth	
1840	03/30/1865	Pickens	Elvin	Ann M.	
1843	02/01/1864	Harnett			
)3/ /1828	7/2/07	Halifax			
1837	2/14/03	Wake			
/02/1847	6/4/23	Burke	William B.	Martha Fullwood	
1844	10/15/12	Currituck	S.L.	Mary	
/11/1838	9/19/23	Pitt	J.R.	Mary E. Jones	
/24/1842	5/14/07	Beaufort	James E.	Mannah	
5/ /1844	12/14/12	Wake			
1830	01/03/1865	Hall	James	Margaret	
1829	05/19/1863	Madison			

D	S	G	RANK	LAST	GIVEN	CO	NR	UNIT
3	1	211	Pvt	Hudson	Junius (CC)	F	43	NC
5	1	337	Pvt	Hudson	William N.(M.)	I	21	Ga Vol Inf
6	1	488	Pvt	Huffman	Jeremiah	C	28	NC
1	1	Arl	Pvt	Hughes	George	I	8	NC
7	3	238	Pvt	Hughs	John M.	H	45	NC
7	1	415	Pvt	Humphrey	James Lee	A	9	Va Cav
4	2	193	Pvt	Hundley	John A.	F	12	NC
6	1	531	Pvt	Hunley	Claiborne P.	A	45	NC
4	1	291	Sgt	Hunsucker	Daniel	G	6	NC Sen Res
7	1	559	Pvt	Hutchins	Andrew Jackson	C	6	NC
1	1	Arl	Pvt	Hyatt	John A.	K	15	NC
8	3	6	Pvt	Hyde	James Thomas	D	10	NC (1 Arty)
8	3	77	Pvt	Hyde	William Harvey	F	29	NC
8	3	42	Pvt	Ingram	John	B	60	NC
6	1	489	Pvt	Iseley	Lewis C.	F	6	NC
4	1	270	Pvt	Jackson	Robert	A		NC Home G
1	1	13	Pvt	Jackson	Shadrack	E	41	NC (3 Cav)
8	3	135	Pvt	Jackson	Thomas	K	51	NC
5	1	344	Pvt	James	John W.	B	41	Ga Vol Inf
4	2	175	Pvt	Jarrett	Benjamin D.	M	16	NC
3	1	105	—	*Jarrett	D. A.	A	32	NC
4	1	273	Pvt	Jean	Nathaniel (CC)	B	47	NC
1	1	Arl	Pvt	Jenkins	Ammon	I	53	NC
1	1	25	Pvt	Jenkins	Docton (CC)	C	11	NC
7	3	331	Pvt	Jenkins	James O.	F	67	NC
7	3	273	Pvt	Jenkins	Robert M.	I	28	NC
7	3	155	Pvt	Jenkins	William M.	I	49	NC
1	2	10	Pvt	Jernigan	William H.	D	23	NC
3	2	147	Sgt	Jewell	William F.	I	40	NC (3 Arty)
5	3	S9	Pvt	Johns	John A.	F	NC	1st Engineer Tr
5	1	325	Pvt	Johnson	B.	B		Ga Phillips'
7	3	173	Pvt	Johnson	George Washington	C	53	NC
3	2	109	Pvt	Johnson	Holley	A	5	NC
3	2	113	Pvt	Johnson	John W. H.	B	12	NC Batt Cav
7	3	259	Pvt	Johnson	Richard F.	E	43	NC
3	1	182	—	*Johnson	W. H.			NC
3	1	236	Pvt	Johnson	W. H. (M)	L	17	NC
5	3	S12	Pvt	Johnson	Wiley T.	C	NC	Fay Ars & Arm
1	1	Arl	Pvt	Johnson	William	F	16	NC
2	1	80	—	*Johnston	(CM)			NC
3	2	50	Pvt	Johnston	John H.	B	44	NC
6	1	444	Pvt	Jolly	Wesley	I	32	NC
2	1	79	Pvt	Jones	Allen	I	44	NC
8	3	15	Pvt	Jones	Alvis C.	D	63	NC (5 Cav)

A Story Behind Every Stone

BIRTH	DEATH	COUNTY	FATHER	MOTHER	WIFE
1845	03/20/1862	Halifax	Charles		
	08/08/1864	Stewart			
1835	10/20/1863	Catawba	Martin	Sarah	
1833	07/09/1864	Alamance			
12/20/1831	5/25/21	Rockingham	John	Nancy	
1845	09/18/1864	Stafford	Charles W.	Matilda	
06/ /1834	9/11/08	Warren	William A.	Mahala	W.
1820	07/17/1863	Rockingham			
1818	02/05/1865	Stanly			Adaline
1833	07/01/1863	Orange		Frances	Elizabeth H. Blalock
1836	08/11/1864	Davidson			
1834	2/4/10	Edgecombe			
1836	1/4/13	Jackson	Benjamin Jr.	Cynthia	
04/ /1835	12/22/11	Buncombe	Joel	Ann	
1846	07/16/1863	Alamance	Lewis	Nancy	
	01/30/1865				
1839	03/21/1865	Pitt	Shadrack	Catherine Sawyer	
1836	5/13/15	Sampson	Henry	Annie Godwin	Priscilla
1822	04/09/1865	Polk			Elizabeth M.
07/ /1839	10/8/07	Gaston	Samuel	Clara	
1827	04/03/1862	Franklin			
1828	06/29/1865	Union	Francis	Dorthea Orme	Serena
1837	04/20/1862	Bertie	Joseph	Ester	
1845	6/12/33	Jones	James	Patsy	
08/04/1838	6/29/27	Yadkin	Coleman O.	Emily E. Orrell	Susan E.
1836	7/2/16	Catawba	Ben	Sallie Heovlin	Margaret
03/15/1843	09/27/1892	Richmond	Samuel C., Jr.	Mary Liles Terry	
1837	10/22/06	Beaufort		Amy	Annie
03/27/1846	8/2/23	Rockingham	James D.	Francis Tensly	
	07/22/1864				
10/24/1845	8/9/17	Johnston	James Moss	Mason Charlotte	
03/ /1839	7/1/04	Chatham			
11/ /1835	12/2/04	Johnston			
11/29/1839	1/9/23	Pitt	Charles R.	Rhodie Crisp	
	../../1865				
12/12/1842	5/26/29	Cumberland	Thomas	Ann	Rachel E. Charles Craft
1840	01/03/1863				
1838	03/30/1898	Martin		Margaret	
1831	08/15/1863	Wilkes	Abel	Fanny	Nancy Cockerham
1833	04/25/1862	Pitt			Fanny
08/ /1840	9/14/10	Orange			Sallie Wray

A Story Behind Every Stone

D	S	G	RANK	LAST	GIVEN	CO	NR	UNIT
1	2	32	Pvt	Jones	Berry J.	K	71	NC (2 Jr Res)
7	3	183	Pvt	Jones	ChristopherColumbus	G	14	Va
6	1	361	Pvt	Jones	David J.	B	33	Miss
6	1	500	Pvt	Jones	Isaac N.	E	45	NC
4	1	272	Pvt	Jones	John W.	D	4	NC Batt Jr Res
8	3	NW1	1st Lt	Jones	Josiah			NC Conscript Ⅾ
1	1	36	Pvt	Jones	McGilbert	G	67	NC
1	1	Arl	Pvt	Jones	Thomas M.	H	45	NC
7	3	163	Pvt	Jordan	Andrew J.	B	16	NC Batt Cav
6	1	466	Pvt	Joyner	James	H	47	NC
4	1	310	Pvt	Joyner	James H.	G	36	NC (2 Arty)
1	2	7	Pvt	Justice	T. M.	E	9	SC
8	3	116	Sgt	Kanoy	Samuel	K	45	NC
6	1	445	Pvt	Keith	Anderson Christopher I	3	NC	1836
8	3	11	Pvt	Keith	Thomas Jefferson	H	7	SC Cav
3	1	212	Pvt	Kelly	John	I	6	NC
7	3	318	Pvt	Kelly	William W.	E	40	NC (3 Arty)
4	1	312	Pvt	Kendrick	Marcus M.	D	71	NC (2 Jr Res)
8	1	423	Pvt	Kennedy	John Thomas	A	6	Fla
4	3	N2	Lt Col	Kennedy	John Thomas		16	NC Batt Cav
5	1	355	Pvt	Kennedy	R. W.	E	22	Ga Siege Arty ᵇ
3	1	115	Pvt	Kerr	Anamander (CC)	E	29	NC
1	1	Arl	2nCorp	Key	Samuel	B	2	NC Batt
7	3	322	Pvt	Kiger	Benjamin Franklin	G	21	NC
8	3	136	Pvt	Kincade	Jacob S.	G	1	NC (6 months)
6	1	469	Capt	Kincaid	James Monroe	G	52	NC
5	3	S11	Pvt	King	Benjamin Franklin	D	1	NC
8	3	114	Music	King	G. W.	D	70	NC (1 Jr Res)
7	3	242	Pvt	King	Jeremiah J.	C	36	NC (2 Arty)
8	3	124	Pvt	King	John H.	A	31	NC
7	3	193	Pvt	King	John W.	D	19	NC (2 Cav)
5	1	342	Pvt	King	Josiah E.	E	27	Ga Batt Inf
7	3	224	Pvt	King	Nathaniel E.	A	14	NC
4	2	196	Pvt	King	Thomas J.	H	41	NC (3 Cav)
5	1	324	Pvt	King	W. G.	F		Ga Phillips' Leg
8	3	87	Pvt	King	Wiley D.	A	60	NC
4	2	212	—	Kingsmore	Richard S.			Ordinance Depⁱ
7	3	311	Pvt	Kinsey	Michael F.	G	56	NC
7	1	419	Pvt	Kirby	Mike	B	10	Tenn
7	3	336	Pvt	Kirby	William C.	H	68	NC
6	1	472	Pvt	Kirkman	Henry Clay Bascom	G	26	NC
8	3	105	Pvt	Kittrell	Robert Kendrick	D	2	NC
3	2	46	Pvt	Knight	Benjamin	H	30	NC
7	3	261	Pvt	Kornegay	James H.	B	52	NC

A Story Behind Every Stone

BIRTH	DEATH	COUNTY	FATHER	MOTHER	WIFE
1847	09/14/1895	Halifax	Simmon	Sarah	
06/20/1839	5/1/18	Halifax	Job	Jane Hall	Mary Frances Hall
1843	03/19/1865	Amite	John	Ellen	
1842	07/04/1863	Rockingham	Isaac	Sarah	
04/22/1847	08/18/1864	Rockingham	J.V.	Margaret	
11/ /1832	5/29/13	Wake	Ransom	Sarah Richards	Mariah F. Woodhouse
1847	04/04/1865	Beaufort	Henry A.		
1827	07/29/1864	Rockingham			Margaret J.
07/31/1835	10/31/16	Edgecombe			Mary Mares
1818	07/01/1863	Wake			Elizabeth
1828	03/20/1865	Brunswick			Lydia (1831)
1822	01/08/1892	Brunswick			
1838	8/31/14	Davidson	Philip	Sophina	Leonore
08/01/1863	Wake			Emily	
02/ /1834	8/7/10	Fairfield		Sarah Shead	Mary
1838	07/05/1863	Wake			
08/16/1845	3/2/30	Robeson	Duncan	Sarah McLaughlin	
1847	01/20/1865	Cleveland	Robert	Cornelia J.	
1839	08/13/1862	Gadsden	Alexander	Helen	
03/05/1824	1/21/13	Wayne	John	Sarah Everett	Elizabeth Ann Pike Cox
	03/25/1865				
1843	12/24/1861	Rutherford	A.O.	Hulda	
1838	09/27/1864	Surry	Linsey	Nancy	
07/11/1841	7/1/31	Stokes	William	Nancy Slaughter	
01/ /1834	5/20/15	Burke			
1838	08/27/1863	Lincoln	G.W.	Barbara	
05/24/1847	6/9/33	Orange	B.F.	Emeline Davis	
01/15/1847	6/27/14	Wake			
11/10/1841	11/26/21	New Hanover	Jeremiah J.	MargaretMcKeough	
06/ /1838	1/5/15	Robeson	David	Susan Blount	
11/05/1833	11/12/18	Cumberland	William H.	Fannie Bird	
1847	03/26/1865	Washington	Josiah J.	Martha C.	
08/26/1847	7/6/20	Halifax	Edward	Susan Harper	
08/ /1831	10/21/08	Onslow	William R.	Winaford	Julia Ann Piner
1824	08/23/1864	Carroll			
11/ /1830	5/10/13	Buncombe	Soloman	Rosanna	
10/ /1839	8/30/09	Wilson			Ann
12/ /1844	12/16/28	Henderson			
	03/30/1865	(Williamson)			
10/18/1848	3/18/35	Hertford			Harriet Hadley
1843	09/01/1863	Chatham	George	Alvey Coble	
1839	3/28/14	Pitt	Allen	Sally Worthington	
1831	03/12/1897	Moore			
08/ /1846	2/16/23	Duplin	Henry	Elva Canady	

D	S	G	RANK	LAST	GIVEN		CO	NR	UNIT
5	3	S8	Pvt	Lacy	George H.		F	27	NC
7	1	412	Pvt	Lamb	A. K.		D	23	SC
2	2	SE4	Pvt	Landis	William T.		B	11	NC
3	1	235	—	*Lanier	Isaac	(CM)			NC
5	1	335	Pvt	Latimer	David F.		C		Ga Phillips' Le
8	3	84	Pvt	Lawrence	George W.		H	22	NC
4	2	173	Pvt	Lawrence	Joseph		G	6	La
8	3	74	Pvt	Laws	John		F	46	NC
3	2	92	Pvt	Lea	Henry		C	41	NC (3 Cav)
7	1	557	Pvt	Leaman	James D.		D	52	NC
7	3	328	Pvt	Leavister	Lorenzo Davis		F	47	NC
1	1	Arl	Pvt	Lee	Richard L.		I	43	NC
1	2	31	Capt	Lee	Thomas G.		D	4	NC
7	3	220	Pvt	Leeson	Stephen Nathaniel		A	19	Va Cav
1	1	22	—	*Legget	James	(CH)			NC
2	1	56	Pvt	Leggett	William E.		D	44	NC
5	1	322	Pvt	Legnin	W. L.		G	5	Ga Vol Inf
3	2	95	Pvt	Leighton	John Henry		E	47	NC
4	1	279	Pvt	Lewis	Alexander		G	36	NC (2 Arty)
3	1	134	—	*Lewis	J.		K		NC
3	1	156	Pvt	Lewis	William A.		B	45	NC
3	1	194	—	*Linden	J. A.				NC
1	1	Arl	Pvt	Lindsay	Richard		I	30	NC
8	3	53	Pvt	Lindsay	Robert G.		D	4	NC Batt'n Jr I
3	2	54	Pvt	Lindsey	William		G	59	NC (4 Cav)
4	1	314	2ndLt	Lineberry	Edwin C.		E	70	NC (1 Jr Res)
8	3	60	Pvt	Lippard	Marcus		D	29	NC
2	1	82	—	*Little	S. W.				NC
7	1	403	Pvt	Livingstone	William J.	(WF)	H	7	SC Batt Inf
1	1	Arl	Pvt	Lloyd	Joseph		B	47	NC
8	3	130	Corp	Long	Hiram		A	3	NC Batt L Ar
4	1	299	Pvt	Long	John W. Jr.		A	13	NC Batt L Ar
2	1	51	—	*Long	L.		B	17	NC
3	2	114	Pvt	Love	Robert		K	13	NC
3	1	112	Pvt	Lowder	Benjamin F.		A	59	NC (4 Cav)
6	1	517	Pvt	Lowder	Jacob W.		B	20	NC
4	1	271	Sgt	Lowman	William A.	(CC)	A	23	NC
1	1	Arl	3rCorp	Lowthrop	Thomas B.		K	43	NC
6	1	477	2nCorp	Luther	Franklin		B	52	NC
1	2	15	Pvt	Lyman	William		D	30	NC
8	3	92	Pvt	Lyons	William		F	37	NC
3	1	183	Pvt	Mabe	Moses		A	2	NC Batt
3	1	160	—	*Macey	C. F.				NC
3	2	84	Pvt	Mahoney	James R.		E	10	NC (1 Arty)

A Story Behind Every Stone

BIRTH	DEATH	COUNTY	FATHER	MOTHER	WIFE
12/29/1838	2/24/23	Perquimans	Thomas	Mary A. White	
	10/24/1862				
1843	08/23/1883	McDowell			Huldah
		Randolph			
1843	08/23/1864	Cobb	Reuben	Sarah	
07/ /1833	3/24/13	Stokes			
08/ /1830	8/5/07				
12/ /1844	10/17/12	Orange	Isaac	Louisa	
1825	1/29/03	Caswell			
1827	07/01/1863	Surry			Ann
09/ /1845	12/14/32	Franklin	George	Louisa	Sarah A.
1846	07/27/1864	Anson	Shepherd	Mary	
1839	08/31/1895	Wilson			
07/20/1846	5/21/20	Wake	John W.	Elizabeth Terry	Martha Rhodes
	09/22/1864				
1842	05/18/1862	Pitt	John	Louisa	
	04/19/1865				
1820	2/27/03	Wake			Mary A.
1842	03/20/1865	Brunswick	Alexander	Lydia Wescott	
	10/24/1862				
	01/20/1863	Alamance			
	04/10/1864				
1831	01/16/1864	Nash	Jeptha	Nancy	
08/ /1846	3/31/12	Rockingham			
1839	06/15/1898	Currituck	William	Angelica	
1847	03/26/1865	Guilford	Orran	Alva	
04/ /1835	5/31/12	Alexander			Susanna Little
1843	04/11/1865	Richmond	John	Margaret	
1824	11/21/1864	Franklin			
1844	4/22/15	Northampton	James F.	Sarah	
1843	11/27/1864	Richmond			
	06/03/1862				
11/09/1821	12/6/04	Rockingham			Leanner
1846	05/01/1864	Stanly	Thomas A.	Catherine	
1841	07/10/1863	Cabarrus	Solomon	Anna M.	
1837	07/10/1861	Anson			
1839	07/13/1864	Anson	Churchwell	Nancy A.	
1840	09/14/1863	Randolph		Mary	
1815	07/15/1893	Granville			Malissa
1843	6/17/13	Surry			
1832	05/10/1863	Stokes	Lewis	Levina	
08/ /1834	6/14/02	New Hanover			

D	S	G	RANK	LAST	GIVEN	CO	NR	UNIT
6	1	460	Pvt	Malloy	John Thomas	E	45	NC
4	2	207	Pvt	Mangum	John S.	A	44	NC
7	3	234	Pvt	Mangum	Peter J.	A	44	NC
7	3	301	Pvt	Manley	William Meridon	I	13	NC
8	1	420	Pvt	Manor	James			Navy
6	1	483	Pvt	Marley	John W.	K	53	NC
1	1	14	Pvt	Marsh	Neill	B	36	NC (2 Art)
1	2	13	Pvt	Marshall	George William	B	2	NC
2	1	86	Pvt	Marshall	John W.	D	59	NC (4 Cav)
7	1	555	Sgt	Marshall	Lauristes L.	E	53	NC
5	3	S7	Pvt	Marshburn	Dr. Henry H.	H	31	NC
1	1	Arl	1st Lt	Martin	Robert M.	A	45	NC
8	3	119	1st Lt	Mason	George N.	C	72	NC (3 Jr Res)
6	1	519	Pvt	Mason	Miles Franklin	G	5	NC
6	1	473	Pvt	Massey	Jacob W.	A	4	NC
3	1	98	—	* Matey	J. L.	I	25	NC
3	1	127	—	* Mathews	John			NC
7	1	394	Pvt	Matthews	John T.	A	5	SC Batt Jr Re
8	3	33	Pvt	May	Thomas M.	E	9	NC (1 Cav)
7	1	559	Sgt	Maynard	John H.	K	6	NC
1	2	18	Pvt	Maynard	William Henry	C	50	NC
7	3	217	Pvt	McBain	Henry G.	H	70	NC (1 Jr Res)
8	3	30	Pvt	McClure	James H.	F	43	NC
1	1	6	Pvt	McCracken	R. H. (CH)	G	35	NC
6	1	533	Capt	McCreery	William Westwood	IG		Pettigrew's Sta
7	1	385	Pvt	McCreight	J. H.	C	3	SC Batt Jr Re
5	1	351	Pvt	McCullough	John Robert (WF)	H	27	Ga Vol Inf
4	1	274	Pvt	McDonald	Augustus A. (WF)	A	8	NC
3	1	170	Pvt	McDonald	Malcolm A.	C	3	NC
1	1	38	Capt	McDugald	William J.			NC McDuga
4	1	268	Pvt	McEachin	S.M.	I	50	NC
5	1	334	Sgt	McElhannon	George W.	H		Ga Cobb's Le
1	1	Arl	Pvt	McFadden	John L.	C	34	NC
6	1	497	Pvt	McGee	Franklin M.	I	32	NC
6	1	542	Pvt	McGrady	Jacob	K	37	NC
7	1	386	Pvt	McKay	James A.	C	1	NC Batt H A
6	1	511	Sgt	McKinney	David	B	2	NC Batt
7	1	559	1stSgt	McKinney	Moses J.	E	6	NC
7	1	391	Pvt	McKinsey	William T. (M)			SC LaFayette L. Art
4	1	248	Pvt	McKoy	H. J.	A	8	NC Sen Res
4	1	284	Pvt	McLain	Alexander C.	I	31	NC
6	1	366	Jr 2Lt	McLaughlin	William J.	H	14	Miss
7	3	283	Pvt	McLean	Joseph M.	M	21	NC
7	3	290	Sgt	McLean	Quincy Clay	D	29	NC

A Story Behind Every Stone

BIRTH	DEATH	COUNTY	FATHER	MOTHER	WIFE
1840	08/12/1863	Rockingham	Daniel/Davil M.		Permilie/Eliz
1833	7/2/09	Granville			
02/07/1834	3/4/21	Granville	John	Martha Hoyd	
05/27/1845	1/12/27	Rockingham	Lanford	Lucinda	Carrie
	01/13/1865				
1835	09/25/1863	Wilkes	Henry	Jane	
1823	03/20/1865	Cumberland	Thomas	Eliza	Caroline
1841	03/30/1893	Wilson	John H.	Nancy W.	Nancy
1831	01/21/1865	Hertford			Emily
1840	07/03/1863	Surry			
04/15/1845	5/1/36	Wake	Lemuel H.	Elizabeth	
1840	08/12/1864	Rockingham			
06/ /1846	9/26/14	Harnett			
1829	07/19/1863	Davie	Richard P.	Martha	Drusey
1840	09/02/1863	Iredell	Ebeneezer	Mahalia Allen	
	../../1865	Richland			
08/31/1831	11/6/11	Franklin			
1834	07/04/1863	Alamance	George	Mary	
1841	01/30/1894	Johnston			Liza
01/31/1844	4/2/20	Chatham	S.D.W.	Mary Inashabush	
1839	8/26/11	Halifax			
1822	01/01/1865	Alamance			
09/ /1836	07/01/1863				
	04/08/1865				
1823	../../1865	Henry			Ruth P.
1840	02/10/1865	Pasquotank			
1840	04/19/1863	Moore	Norman	Ann	
1845	04/01/1865	Bladen	Coll	Lucy A.	
	12/19/1864	Rutherford			
	08/11/1864	Jackson			Mary Trout
1846	07/21/1864	Rutherford		Cynthia	
1841	07/11/1863	Wilkes			Mitelly
1834	07/14/1863	Ashe			Jane
1847	04/09/1865	Columbus	Jabez	Ann E.	
1842	07/01/1863	Surry	Fountain	Martha	
1837	07/ /1863	Yancey		Elya M.	
1847	03/07/1865	Beaufort	John E.	Rachael	
	12/30/1864				
1834	01/06/1864	Harnett		Mary	
1843	04/26/1865	Lauderdale			
02/07/1840	9/17/25	Guilford	John	Eliz Thorn	
1844	2/17/26	Madison			

D	S	G	RANK	LAST	GIVEN	CO	NR	UNIT
8	3	106	Pvt	McLendon	John C.	B	43	NC
4	1	305	Pvt	McMillen	James	H	72	NC (3 Jr Res)
7	3	154	Pvt	McNeil	Daniel	H	46	NC
8	3	8	1st Lt	McNeill	Kenneth M.	F	15	NC
4	2	189	Pvt	McQueen	James Donahoe	F	18	NC
1	2	37	Pvt	Meeks	Henry	B	2	NC
3	2	121	Pvt	Melson	John A.	C	19	NC (2 Cav)
7	3	306	Pvt	Melton	Atlas D.	I	52	NC
1	1	19	Pvt	Melton	Burrell T.	B	41	NC (3 Cav)
3	2	105	Pvt	Melvin	Robert Daniel	I	51	NC
8	3	103	Pvt	Mercer	Stephen C.	A	31	NC
8	3	129	Pvt	Merritt	George H.	K	44	NC
7	3	307	Pvt	Merritt	Lewis W.	C	51	NC
7	3	206	Music	Millard	Kenan	E	20	NC
4	1	245	Pvt	Miller	David	H	56	NC
7	3	329	Pvt	Miller	Henry			Signal Corp-Hampton
2	1	47	Pvt	Miller	John B.	B	48	NC
8	2	N6	Pvt	Miller	John F.	K	14	NC
4	1	242	Pvt	Miller	John Silas	H	35	NC
6	1	493	Corp	Miller	John T.(W.)	E	45	NC
1	1	Arl	Pvt	Miller	Joseph	C	57	NC
4	2	178	Pvt	Miller	Joseph A.	D	5	NC
7	2	345	Pvt	Mills	Wiley J.	D	26	NC
4	1	301	Pvt	Mitchell	Edward D.	G	31	NC
1	1	Arl	Pvt	Mitchell	Eli M.	G	44	NC
6	1	498	Pvt	Mitchell	Thomas J.	G	32	NC
8	1	435	Pvt	Monohan	Partrick	H	17	Ala
8	1	437	Pvt	Montgomery	Hugh (Flowlet's Farm)	E	11	Texas Cav
8	3	145	Pvt	Moody	Julius S.	C	68	NC
7	3	160	Pvt	Moore	Abram B.	E	23	SC Inf
6	1	506	Pvt	Moore	George W.	F	6	NC
8	3	23	Pvt	Moore	George W.	K	17	NC
1	1	Arl	Pvt	Moore	James T.	G	45	NC
4	1	306	Pvt	Moore	John W.	C	41	NC (3 Cav)
4	2	198	Pvt	Moore	Marion Thadeous	D	72	NC (3 Jr Res)
7	3	246	Pvt	Moore	William R.	H	4	NC
8	3	123	Music	Moore	William W.	H	1	NC
3	2	134	Sgt	Mooring	John	E	17	NC
3	1	231	Pvt	Morgan	George	F	26	NC
5	1	354	Pvt	Morgan	J. H.		3	Ga Art
7	3	235	Pvt	Morgan	Permenter B.	K	22	NC
8	3	58	Pvt	Morris	Benjamin J.	E	8	NC
2	1	53	Pvt	Morris	Daniel	D	48	NC
1	1	Arl	Pvt	Morris	James	F	7	NC

A Story Behind Every Stone

BIRTH	DEATH	COUNTY	FATHER	MOTHER	WIFE
06/ /1842	3/29/14	Anson	Louis	Ann	
1847	02/24/1865	Cumberland	Neill	Racheal Bane	
05/ /1834	6/30/16	Moore	Daniel	Prattilda Britt	
6 Sep 1834	7/16/10	Harnett	Daniel A.	Rachel Murchison	
01/ /1842	5/30/08	Richmond			
1820	01/22/1896	Wilson			Temperance
1823	3/11/05	Tyrrell	William	Olive Pledger	Ann B.
07/08/1846	9/30/27	Stanly	Joseph D.	Clementine	Mary F.
1839	02/21/1865	Onslow	Geo. Washington		Elizabeth Morse
1834	3/15/04	Bladen	Arthur T.	Charlotte Averitt	Molsey Fisher
1845	3/14/14	Robeson			
01/ /1842	4/21/15	Franklin			
02/19/1839	3/5/28	Pender	Caspert		
11/04/1843	6/1/19	Wayne	Bennett	Sarah Bask	
1832	05/11/1864	Alexander		Elizabeth	
01/28/1844	2/14/33	Scotland	Henry F.	Nancy Kirk	
1832	04/18/1865	Davidson	Jacob	Mary	
		Wake			
	01/02/1862	Meckenburg			
1843	07/20/1863	Rockingham		Elizabeth	
1825	05/06/1865	Rowan			
08/ /1838	11/26/07	Lenoir			
08/26/1834	03/17/1897	Wake	Mathew	Piety	
05/11/1841	03/26/1865	Hertford	James	Mary	
1840	04/21/1865	Alamance	Randal	Nancy	
1837	07/08/1863	Bertie			
	04/07/1865				
1840		Red River			
04/28/1846	2/5/16	Wake	William	Susan Malow	
05/12/1839	8/28/16	Robeson	Abram	Emma Thompsons	
1842	07/04/1863	Orange	John	Henrietta	
1829	3/12/11	Pitt			
1842	08/19/1864	Rockingham			
1832	02/21/1865	Caswell	William W.	Sarah	
1847	11/24/08	Pender	Alfred M.	Anna J.	
1843	1/5/22	Iredell	William	Malinda Morris	Louisa
1844	12/28/14	Martin			
02/ /1842	2/4/06	Martin	A.S.	Martha	
1837	07/30/1863	Caldwell			
	02/22/1865				
07/10/1836	3/4/21	McDowell	Wilson	Rebecca	
1835	5/12/12	Harnett			
1834	05/14/1862	Moore	Stephen	Janet	
1843	05/30/1864	Davidson	William P.	Anne	

D	S	G	RANK	LAST	GIVEN	CO	NR	UNIT
1	1	Arl	Pvt	Morris	William C.	E	4	NC
7	3	181	QtrMst	Morrison	Elam F.		4	NC Field & Sta
8	3	94	Pvt	Moseley	Gabriel H.	E	20	NC
3	2	81	Pvt	Munce	John	I	36	NC (2 Arty)
8	3	56	Pvt	Murphy	Richard R.	A	42	Va
4	2	156	Pvt	Murray	Jackson	I	8	NC
4	2	168	Pvt	Myrick	George Badger	E	44	NC
7	3	303	Pvt	Nash	George W.	B	22	NC
4	2	216	2nd Lt	Neal	Oscar M.	M	15	NC
4	2	206	Pvt	Nelson	James O.	I	19	NC (2 Cav)
1	1	Arl	Pvt	Nethercutt	Loftin	B	3	NC
8	3	4	Pvt	Neville	Robert O.	A	12	Va
7	3	200	Pvt	Nevills	John F.	A	44	NC
2	2	SE5	Corp	Newby	William H.	K	32	NC
8	3	2	Pvt	Nichols	Martin S.	G	13	NC
1	1	Arl	Pvt	Nipper	James H.	E	47	NC
3	2	52	Pvt	Nolan	Patrick A.	A	10	NC (1 Arty)
5	1	328	Pvt	Nolinson	Daniel	H	49	Ga Vol Inf
7	3	219	Pvt	Norment	John Jackson	A	11	NC
8	1	436	Capt	Norris	Thomas (Chapel Hill)	F	3	Ala Cav
7	1	553	Pvt	Nowell	Ransom Green	K	14	NC
2	1	77	Pvt	Nurney	Nathan Henry	C	17	NC
8	3	144	Pvt	Nutt	Guilford	D	56	NC
4	1	295	Pvt	Oakley	D.	E	6	NC Home Gu
4	2	148	Pvt	O'Brien	Alexander B.	L	22	NC
8	3	NW2	Pvt	O'Daniel	James H.	C	47	NC
3	2	104	Sgt	Oden	James A.	B	17	NC
3	1	185	Pvt	Oder	William A. (CC)	C	3	NC Batt L Art
8	3	100	Pvt	Oliver	Daniel	H	59	NC (4 Cav)
7	3	270	Pvt	O'Neal	Matthew	F	33	NC
7	3	164	Pvt	Orr	Matthew L.	K	62	NC
3	2	98	Pvt	Orrell	Joseph N.	G	23	NC
3	1	161	Pvt	Overby	Robert H.	G	10	NC (1 Arty)
7	3	190	Pvt	Overcash	Otho C.	I	7	NC
3	2	107	Pvt	Overcash	Solomon Wiley	G	42	NC
3	2	117	Pvt	Overton	George Campton	G	47	NC
7	3	213	Pvt	Pace	Edward	F	6	NC
1	1	Arl	Pvt	Page	Bryant	I	51	NC
7	3	341	Pvt	Page	Marion Dempsey	D	40	NC (3 Arty)
2	1	48	Pvt	Page	Robert	B	8	NC
7	3	335	Pvt	Palmer	Joseph M.	A	22	NC
5	1	326	Pvt	Park	Byrd	L		Ga Cobb's Legion Cav
8	3	82	Pvt	Parker	Stephen R.	C	54	NC
3	2	41	Pvt	Parker	Weeks B.	A	10	NC (1 Arty)

A Story Behind Every Stone

BIRTH	DEATH	COUNTY	FATHER	MOTHER	WIFE
1840	06/02/1864	Craven			Elander
04/14/1838	4/12/18	Iredell	Sander W.	Jane C. Cowan	Mary Eliza Summers
07/ /1841	9/13/13	Sampson	James M.	Sarah Elizabeth Hobbs	
08/ /1821	4/2/02	Bladen			I.B.
1836	4/26/12	Forsyth			
10/ /1824	3/13/07	Alamance			Lena
1832	7/5/07	Chatham			
08/ /1847	3/6/27	Buncombe			
12/ /1832	10/31/09	Chatham	John	Martha A.	
05/ /1835	6/17/09	Moore			
1839	02/10/1864	Duplin	John	Elizabeth	Cathrine
03/ /1837	1/6/10	Buncombe			
01/07/1844	1/5/19	Granville	Jim	Sallie Mangum	
1840	03/29/1883	Franklin			
04/ /1838	11/17/09	Yadkin		Nancy	
1834	12/30/1863	Wake			Phoebie Turner Allen
1837	11/02/1898	Edgecombe			
	07/23/1862	Washington			
10/30/1841	5/17/20	Mecklenburg	John	Annie Willis	
1841	04/17/1865	Perry	William J.	R. Louisiana	
1/15/1842	07/01/1863	Wake	James	Mary Ann Shaw	
1842	06/08/1862	Hertford		Martha	
1829	12/26/15	Orange			Lethe
	01/13/1865				
02/ /1837	10/26/06	Randolph	Mial	Jane	
10/ /1839	5/30/16	Wake	Green	Kitty Goodwin	
01/ /1836	2/17/04	Beaufort			
1821	04/03/1862	Bertie		Mary	
06/ /1813	2/24/14	Wilson			Amanda
07/ /1836	3/9/24	Hyde			
06/ /1838	10/31/16	Henderson	Robert	Margaret	Sarah
03/ /1841	3/29/03	Granville		Franky	
1828	03/04/1864	Granville	Ahab	Agness	Panthea
9/11/1833	8/15/18	Iredell	Michael	Margaret	
04/ /1833	5/10/04	Rowan	Francis	Mary Beaver	
1844	1/12/05	Granville	Arthur A.	Jane	
3/12/1832	2/19/20	Alamance	Joseph	Eliza	
1847	09/03/1864	Cumberland		Elizabeth	
6/28/1846	9/25/36	Edgecombe	Johnston	Lydia Gardner	nm
	04/17/1865	Cabarrus			
2/15/1845	1/25/35	Caswell			
	08/16/1864				
03/ /1845	3/13/13	Cumberland	Thomas R.	Charity Bedsole	
1845	05/11/1896	Edgecombe	Simmons B.	Emily Ann	Ann Pitt

D	S	G	RANK	LAST	GIVEN	CO	NR	UNIT
3	2	44	Pvt	Parker	William H.	F	10	NC (1 Arty)
3	2	56	Pvt	Parker	William Howel	H	27	NC
6	1	470	Pvt	Parrish	Uriah R.	I	19	NC (2 Cav)
7	1	439	Sgt	Parsons	William Holt	K	12	Va Mahone's
2	1	54	Pvt	Partin	Alexander (M)	A	68	NC
2	1	75	Pvt.	Partin	C.C.	C	3	NC Batt L A
7	3	167	Pvt	Paschall	Richard B.	G	43	NC
5	1	323	Pvt	Pate	John A.	B	10	Ga Batt Inf
5	1	321	Pvt	Patrick	Dennis M.	F	10	Ga Cav
7	1	416	Pvt	Payne	James K.	H	8	Va
7	1	401	Pvt	Payne	Joseph F.	K	2	SC Inf
4	1	239	Pvt	Peal	Turner	H	26	NC
7	3	314	Pvt	Pearcy	J. W.	B	11	NC
3	2	144	Pvt	Pechel	Solomon	G	42	NC
1	1	Arl	Pvt	Peebles	William	D	44	NC
7	3	271	Pvt	Peel	Lawrence	F	40	NC (3 Arty)
1	1	Arl	Pvt	Pendergrast	Robert W.	G	43	NC
6	1	480	1stSgt	Pendley	Merrit B.	E	6	NC
1	1	7	Pvt	Perdue	William	G	40	NC (3 Arty)
7	1	383	Pvt	Perry	Daniel	C	27	SC
7	3	293	Pvt	Perry	James R.	F	31	NC
6	1	485	Pvt	Perry	Joseph E.	G	32	NC
4	1	258	Conscr	Perry	Peter			NC
3	1	191	—	* Person	L. W.	F	25	NC
3	2	71	Pvt	Pettitt	Benjamin F.	C	16	NC Batt Cav
4	2	184	Pvt	Petty	Winship S.	E	63	NC (5 Cav)
6	1	463	Pvt	Pfeiffer	Jacob	E	40	NY
8	3	41	Pvt	Phelps	Bailey	G	18	NC
7	3	184	Pvt	Phillips	John	I	22	NC
3	1	133	Pvt	Phillips	John W.	H	43	Miss
7	3	192	Pvt	Phillips	Leonidas	A	27	NC
2	1	65	Pvt	Phillips	McKinney	H	48	NC
4	2	163	Pvt	Phillips	Thomas B.	A	27	NC
7	3	323	Pvt	Phipps	Francis Marion	F	8	Va
1	2	36	Pvt	Pierce	Christopher C.	H	10	NC (1 Arty)
4	2	197	Pvt	Pierce	John	H	27	NC
3	1	187	Pvt	Pilkinton	Joseph A.	D	61	NC
6	1	478	Pvt	Pittman	Benjamin F.	C	1	NC
4	2	174	Pvt	Pittman	James A.	F	47	NC
6	1	364	Pvt	Pittman	John	I	3	Miss
8	3	85	Pvt	Plummer	Alfred A.	F	12	NC
1	2	14	Pvt	Poe	William	M	15	NC
1	1	Arl	Pvt	Pointer	Haywood	A	24	NC
4	2	211	Pvt	Pool	James K.	D	31	NC

A Story Behind Every Stone

BIRTH	DEATH	COUNTY	FATHER	MOTHER	WIFE
1827	07/20/1896	Gates			Emma D.
1830	10/27/1899	Pitt			
11/11/1837	08/30/1863	Moore	Blakley	Anna Christian	
1842	01/09/1864				
	04/08/1863				
	1864				
1842	1/9/17	Warren	I.B.	Mary	
	08/14/1864				
1835	04/18/1865	Chatham			
	12/20/1864				
1837	10/21/1862				
1835	04/23/1865	Martin	Dennis	Edna Rogerson	
1838	2/2/29	Catawba			
08/ /1825	9/11/06	Rowan			
1844	12/30/1863	Pitt	Howell	Clary	
03/ /1844	7/3/24	Edgecombe		Lydia	
1832	03/28/1865	Warren			
1830	09/18/1863	Burke			
1816	04/05/1865	Lenoir			Mary
1822	03/24/1865	Fairfield			Mary
04/03/1842	6/23/26	Martin	John	Margaret Hodge	
1845	09/27/1863	Bertie	Augustus	Jane	
	04/15/1864				
	03/17/1865				
1845	7/26/01	Halifax	William	Lucinda Hart	
1835	7/9/08	Chatham	Stephen	Martha	Eliza A. Clark
1846	08/11/1863	NY City	Joseph	Caroline Leies	
10/ /1830	12/16/11	Washington	Micajah	Eveline	Nancy
1840	5/8/18	Randolph			Eliza
1835	01/04/1865	Itawamba			Minerva
09/29/1845	10/21/18	Greene	Henry	Emiline Bond	
1836	05/20/1862	Davidson			
11/ /1834	5/19/07	Wayne	Lewis H.	Eveline	
09/26/1843	10/15/31	Wilkes	Samuel	Grace Daughan	
1832	12/19/1895	Carteret			
06/ /1843	10/23/08	Lenoir			
1833	12/29/1862	Chatham			Malinda I.
1835	09/14/1863	Johnston	Garry	Martha	Lany
1833	9/18/07	Franklin			Pricilla G. May
	10/12/1865	Marion			
1838	3/25/13	Warren	Henry Lyne	Sara Falkener	
1820	05/30/1893	Chatham	Ransom	Anna	
1844	04/13/1865	Person	Joseph	Susan Adams	
06/ /1843	8/30/09	Wake			

A Story Behind Every Stone

D	S	G	RANK	LAST	GIVEN	CO	NR	UNIT
8	3	61	Pvt	Poole	John M.	E	14	NC
4	2	194	Pvt	Pope	Albert S.	I	41	NC (3 Cav)
8	3	63	Pvt	Pope	Alexander C.	H	3	NC
5	1	343	Corp	Pope	John Clark	E	42	Ga Vol Inf
1	1	Arl	Pvt	Porter	George Thomas	I	43	NC
7	3	239	Pvt	Posey	Benjamin M.	G	56	NC
7	1	396	2ndLt	Powell	A. D.	M	5	SC Inf
4	2	180	Pvt	Powell	Josiah J.	C	41	NC (3 Cav)
3	2	63	Pvt	Powell	William D.	G	1	NC (6 month
7	3	342	Pvt	Powers	Robert Patrick	K	72	NC (3 Jr Res)
2	1	74	—	* Price	D. R. (CM)			NC
8	3	104	1st Lt	Price	Thomas A.	A	6	NC
3	2	E4	Pvt	Price	William L.	E	17	NC
1	2	6	Pvt	Prince	John	D	26	NC
3	2	79	Pvt	Puckett	James H.	B	19	NC (2 Cav)
8	3	107	Pvt	Puckett	John W.	G	1	NC
3	2	E1	Pvt	Pugh	David	E	47	NC
8	3	122	Pvt	Purser	Jesse D.	B	40	NC (3 Arty)
8	3	79	Sgt	Purvis	John R.	B	33	NC
4	2	157	Pvt	Puryear	John R.	I	23	NC
7	3	312	Pvt	Pyatt	James A.	B	22	NC
7	3	228	Pvt	Quartermast	James Benjamin, Sr.	H	27	NC
8	3	44	Pvt	Quinton	John T.	M	1	NC (6 month
7	3	153	Pvt	Rainey	Josiah R.	G	27	NC
3	2	127	Surg'n	Ramseur	David P.	.	14	NC
6	1	541	Pvt	Ramsey	W. F.	A	10	NC (1 Arty)
4	2	176	Music	Ransdell	George W.	K	32	NC
2	1	87	Pvt	Rathbone	John Hiram (CC)	E	29	NC
3	1	96	Pvt	Rawls	Joseph R. (M)	H	17	NC
7	3	178	Pvt	Rea	Pinkney Caldwell	C	10	NC Batt H A
1	1	Arl	Pvt	Reaves	Samuel F.	D	20	NC
7	3	334	Pvt	Redwine	Greenberry Osborn	B	71	NC (2 Jr Res)
4	1	307	Pvt	Reed	Charles (CC)	H	29	NC
1	1	11	—	* Reeves	L.			NC
7	3	218	Pvt	Register	Joseph J.	D	67	NC
6	1	461	Sgt	Reid	Calvin H.	F	7	NC
4	1	N4	Lt	Reid	Joseph J.	A		NC Mallett's
1	1	Arl	Pvt	Reinhardt	Levi	F	23	NC
7	1	393	Pvt	Reseman	G. W.	D	1	SC Batt Jr Re
3	1	209	Pvt	Rhodes	Battle	I	10	NC (1 Arty)
1	1	24	Pvt	Rhyne	George Richardson	C	71	NC (2 Jr Res
8	3	21	Capt	Richardson	Joseph C.	C	53	NC
6	1	536	2nd Lt	Richardson	William W.	B	26	NC
7	3	302	Pvt	Riddle	William M.	G	63	NC (5 Cav)

A Story Behind Every Stone

BIRTH	DEATH	COUNTY	FATHER	MOTHER	WIFE
03/01/1812	6/2/12	Wake			
10/ /1840	10/1/08	Wake	Silas	Elizabeth	
1844	7/6/12	Randolph			
1831	04/01/1865	Jasper			Emily C.
1829	06/13/1864	Anson			Caroline Throgmorton
08/01/1844	6/9/21	Buncombe	Williamson	Rochel Murray	
	03/12/1865				
11/ /1828	12/18/07	Caswell			
09/ /1838	8/17/00	Burke			Adeline
1847	12/9/37	Rockingham	William H.	Nancy	
10/ /1835	3/27/14	Rowan			
04/ /1844	5/17/06	Martin			
1822	01/01/1892	Wake	John	Nancy Spence	Mary
12/ /1831	3/8/02	Iredell	John P.	Catharine F.	
02/ /1838	4/16/14	Gaston			M.A.
1809	11/06/1897	Wake			
1821	12/22/14	Beaufort	Jesse	Elizabeth Lane	Sarah B. Caten
06/ /1841	2/17/13	Pitt			
02/ /1831	4/4/07	Granville	Peyton	Frances Amis	
05/15/1846	1/20/29	McDowell	Davis	Caroline	
11/01/1839	10/6/20	Beaufort	James Thomas	Ruth Roundtree	Elizabeth A. Neumans
06/ /1840	12/31/11	Chowan			
07/ /1844	6/6/16	Caswell	James Glenn	Sophia Hendrick	
04/14/1839	7/5/05	Lincoln	Jacob A.	Lucy Dodson	
1838	07/02/1863	Wake			
07/ /1835	11/2/07	Franklin			
1844	11/29/1861	Haywood	Wesley	Cassender	
1838	../../1865	Martin	Dennis	Martha	
08/27/1843	3/13/18	Union	John M.	Mary Ritchie	
1832	05/20/1864	Columbus			
01/09/1847	9/25/34	Rowan	Green	Catherine Cauble	
1842	11/17/1861	Buncombe			Christiana (1842)
	10/08/1864				
09/10/1841	4/3/20	Lenoir	Gus Suggs	Everline Register	
1841	08/13/1863	Davidson			
01/10/1837	12/13/1862	Henderson			
18 Jun 1826	05/30/1864	Catawba	David	Mary Mason	Mary Ann Seitz
	11/29/1865				
1830	01/30/1864	Wake	John	Rebecca	Harriett
01/20/1846	02/09/1865	Gaston	David	Malinda S. Fite	
03/ /1840	1/26/11	Durham			
1837	07/01/1863	Union	William Phillip		Nancy
12/24/1838	2/19/27	Chatham	Barney	Nancy Ellington	

A Story Behind Every Stone

D	S	G	RANK	LAST	GIVEN	CO	NR	UNIT
4	1	289	—	* Rivenbrick	G.	C	68	NC
4	2	171	Pvt	Roark	William B.	A	9	NC (1 Cav)
4	2	214	Pvt	Robbins	Starkey	K	15	NC
8	3	88	Pvt	Roberts	James W.	K	4	NC
8	1	427	SgtMaj	Robertson	Francis	A	1	Ark Mntd Rifle
6	1	442	Pvt	Robertson	James	B	45	NC
3	2	146	Pvt	Robertson	William M.	K	21	NC
6	1	476	Corp	Robinson	Joseph B.	G	52	NC
4	2	215	2nd Lt	Robinson	Thomas W.	K	18	NC
8	3	140	Pvt	Roe	Winfield S.	K	71	NC (2 Jr Res)
1	1	Arl	Pvt	Rogers	Samuel S.	B	15	NC
4	1	243	Pvt	Rolland	S. R.	C	55	Ga Vol Inf
6	1	528	Sgt	Rollins	James J.	H	28	NC
6	1	538	2nd Lt	Roney	Lemuel H.	I	57	NC
7	3	171	Corp	Ross	Samuel R.	K	17	NC (2nd co)
8	3	70	Pvt	Rowland	Theophilus T.	G	43	NC
3	1	99	—	* Royston	J. L.	C	25	NC
3	1	203	Pvt	Ruffin	Gray	F		NC Mallett's B
7	3	205	Pvt	Ryland	Noah	F	40	NC (3 Arty)
1	1	Arl	Pvt	Sailor	Joseph W.	K	48	NC
8	3	37	Pvt	Salmon	Sidney	G	40	NC (3 Arty)
7	3	157	Pvt	Sams	Robert R.	D	29	NC
8	3	86	Pvt	Sandlin	Jesse L.	A	38	NC
1	2	3	Pvt	Sanford	John W.	F	47	NC
8	3	64	Pvt	Sanford	Robert H.	H	1	NC (6 months)
3	1	113	Pvt	Sasser	Eli	H	51	NC
3	1	92	Pvt	Sasser	James	A	45	Ga Vol Inf
7	3	199	Pvt	Sauls	Rufus A.	E	10	NC (1 Arty)
7	3	208	Pvt	Saunders	Robert J.	H	5	NC
7	3	254	Pvt	Savage	Calvin N., Jr.	E	17	NC
6	1	360	2nd Lt	Savage	Robert M.	D	23	Miss
3	2	86	Pvt	Scarlett	James Sidney	E	13	NC Batt L Art
5	1	340	Pvt	Schronder	G. W.	B	2	Ga Batt Res
6	1	363	Pvt	Scott	Joseph H.	B	3	Miss
7	3	285	Pvt	Scott	William D.	D	13	NC
6	1	543	Pvt	* Scruggs	J.	D	16	NC
7	1	440	—	* Scumpart	G. W.		1	SC
4	2	205	Pvt	Sealey	Neverson	D	1	NC Batt H Ar
1	2	28	Pvt	Sealey	Wiley A.	A	31	NC
7	3	177	Pvt	Sealy	Allen H.	A	31	NC
5	1	352	Pvt	Sealy	Robert Thomas (WF)	G	27	Ga Vol Inf
1	2	19	Pvt	Sears	Charles E.	I	7	Conf Cav
4	2	188	Pvt	Sechrist	Henry	H	48	NC
7	3	288	Pvt	Sellers	William (Pink)	E	6	NC

A Story Behind Every Stone

BIRTH	DEATH	COUNTY	FATHER	MOTHER	WIFE
	03/18/1865				
12/ /1835	7/9/07	Ashe	Timothy	Susannah	
1834	9/6/09	Edgecombe	Isaac	Catherine Daws	Elizabeth Flood
05/ /1840	5/16/13	Davidson	Stephen	Alice C.	
1837	03/29/1865	Chicot			
1824	08/14/1863	Rockingham			Sarah
03/ /1840	10/12/06	Forsyth	David	Catherine	
1841	09/09/1863	Lincoln		Rosannah	O.
06/ /1832	9/6/09	Bladen	James Sen	Sarah A.	
12/ /1844	6/24/15	Franklin	William	Elizabeth	
1839	02/29/1864	Union	Rushing	Mary	
	03/19/1865				
1834	07/22/1863	Cleveland	Jonas	Mary	
1830	07/01/1863	Alamance	Andrew Jackson		Sarah Freeman
10/10/1837	5/3/17	Pitt	Dovis	Rachel Gaines	
06/ /1841	9/7/12	Warren	Robert	Julia	
	01/10/1864				
1828	10/12/1863	Halifax	Duncan Lamon	Theresa White	Mourning Winstead
)4/04/1833	5/23/19	Greene	James	Peggie Andrews	
1845	10/01/1865	Forsyth			
09/ /1840	11/24/11	Chatham			
01/ /1836	8/14/16	Madison	John	Sallie Blackwell	
1841	3/27/13	Duplin	Robert	Martha	
1840	12/02/1891	Wake			
02/ /1832	7/9/12	Cumberland			
1818	01/10/1863	Columbus			Helen
	04/24/1863	Bibb			
)6/14/1840	12/31/18	Chatham	Abner	... Horten	Eliza
)4/05/1841	9/10/19	Gates	Gilbert G.	Nancy Williams	
)4/10/1845	11/2/22	Edgecombe	Warren	Ruth Cutchin	
1841	03/31/1865	Tishomingo		Rosanna	
1844	7/18/02	Orange	Page	Sally	Susan H.
	04/07/1865				
	04/26/1865	Sunflower			
)4/03/1842	10/11/25	Person	James	Annie Dixon	
1843	07/22/1863				
	09/18/1862				
11/ /1846	6/9/09	Robeson	Willie	Selah	
1822	03/16/1895	Robeson			
6/15/1844	2/28/18	Robeson	James	Adaline Walters	
1842	04/06/1865	Pike	Peter B.	Eleanor W.	
1830	05/09/1894	Nash			Delphia D.
03/ /1843	4/23/08	Davidson	Jonathan	Rachael	
8/11/1830	1/22/26	Buncombe	Joseph P.	Vina Tate	

A Story Behind Every Stone

D	S	G	RANK	LAST	GIVEN		CO	NR	UNIT
5	1	353	Pvt	Sesnos	J. S.		E	27	Ga Vol Inf
7	1	382	Pvt	Sexton	James		E	3	SC Batt Jr R
7	3	229	Corp	Shaver	Pleasant Augustus		A	4	NC
3	2	88	Pvt	Shaw	Daniel P.		B	18	NC
3	1	198	Pvt	Shaw	Thomas B.		H	26	NC
7	3	212	Pvt	Shaw	William W.		K	41	NC (3 Cav)
3	1	147	—	*Shea	J. W.		I	25	NC
7	3	227	Pvt	Shea	Thomas		I	13	NC
1	1	37	Pvt	Shearley	William	(CC)	F	43	NC
1	2	33	Lands	Sheffield	James M.				Navy *Virgin*
3	1	176	—	*Shella	T. H.			50	NC
7	3	279	Pvt	Shepard	George W.		K	3	NC
7	3	333	Pvt	Shephard	John J.		D	36	NC (2 Arty)
1	1	Arl	Pvt	Shepherd	James, Jr.		G	3	NC
3	2	66	Pvt	Shepherd	William R.		K	49	NC
4	2	186	Pvt	Shinalt	Benjamin J.		H	21	NC
1	2	29	Pvt	Short	James E.		E	48	NC
5	2	S15	Capt	Shotwell	Randolph Abbott		I	8	Va Vol
4	2	210	Capt	Siler	Columbus Frank		M	22	NC
8	3	131	Pvt	Sills	Henry Washington		K	51	NC
8	3	1	Corp	Simms	Daniel E.		H	51	NC
3	1	123	Pvt	Simpson	J. D.		I	27	NC
1	1	28	Pvt	Simpson	John P.		F	71	NC (2 Jr Re
5	1	318	Pvt	Simpson	T. E.				Ga Macon
1	1	Arl	2nCorp	Singletary	Travis W.		B	18	NC
1	1	Arl	Pvt	Sisk	William F.		G	54	NC
3	1	93	—	*Slider	Lemuel			27	NC
7	3	300	Pvt	Sloan	George W.		D	35	NC
7	3	245	Pvt	Smith	Alexander		G	21	NC
7	3	214	Pvt	Smith	Alexander L.				NC McDugald's Com
8	3	78	Pvt	Smith	Balthrop		D	12	NC (2nd cc
3	1	215	Pvt	Smith	Basil T.		E	44	NC
4	1	276	Pvt	Smith	Calvin		I	66	NC
3	2	140	Pvt	Smith	James A.		C	53	NC
1	1	Arl	Pvt	Smith	James W. S.		H	48	NC
8	3	97	Seaman	Smith	John E.				Navy NC
4	1	311	Pvt	Smith	John W.		K	61	NC
7	3	182	Pvt	Smith	John W.		C	36	NC (2 Art)
7	3	179	Pvt	Smith	Joseph W.		E	1	Miss Batt C
1	1	Arl	Pvt	Smith	Josiah S.		H	20	NC
1	1	15	Pvt	Smith	Loften				NC McDugald's Com
8	3	31	Pvt	Smith	Moses L.		A	42	NC
7	3	221	Pvt	Smith	Nathan		I	17	NC
4	2	203	Pvt	Smith	S. Logan		B	57	NC

A Story Behind Every Stone

BIRTH	DEATH	COUNTY	FATHER	MOTHER	WIFE
	03/02/1865	Campbell			
	03/25/1865				
08/12/1838	10/16/20	Iredell	Sam	Elizabeth Sloan	
09/ /1835	9/2/02	Bladen	Duncan	Mary Formyduval	
1830	10/06/1864	Moore			
03/11/1840	1/24/20	Beaufort	Mathrew	Hannah Bonner	
	04/20/1863				
08/01/1830	9/14/20	Guilford	John H.	Mary O'Leary	
1837	../../1862	Halifax	Bird	Losanna	
1827	10/09/1895	Mecklenburg			
02/ /1844	7/2/25	New Hanover			
04/08/1847	7/8/34	New Hanover	Thomas	Betsy Rhodes	
1835	01/07/1864	Onslow	James	Mary	
12/ /1844	1/14/01	Gaston			
1838	3/29/08	Surry			
1844	03/18/1895	Union	John	Nancy	
12/13/1843	07/31/1885		Nathan		
12/ /1840	7/28/09	Randolph	Andrew J.	Ruth	
1845	4/23/15	Sampson	David	Sarah A.	Seereny
02/ /1831	9/26/09	Robeson			
	11/04/1862	Jones			
11/20/1846	02/07/1865				
	../../1864				
1835	01/13/1865	Bladen	Jesse	Catherine	
1841	03/04/1864	Wilkes	Harrison	Dicey	
	07/02/1862				
05/20/1840	10/15/26	Chatham	Robert	Nancy Marks	
07/17/1833	12/21/21	Stokes	Solomon	Peggie Hastings	Nancy
01/13/1847	2/24/20	Sampson	John R.	Sarah A. Lamb	
11/ /1843	2/6/13	Granville	Bourborn	MargaretRoberson	
1825	01/24/1864	Chatham		Fanny	Martha A. (1831)
1829	07/05/1864	Lenoir		Mithina	Alice
11/ /1831	9/5/06	Wake			Vicy
1842	05/03/1865	Davidson			
1845	1/11/14	Granville	Bouborn	Margaret Roberson	
1846	03/26/1865	Lenoir			
11/15/1835	4/23/18	Wake	Randolph	Jane C. Wilder	
07/04/1835	3/19/18	Jackson			
1832	06/11/1864	Sampson			
	02/03/1865	New Hanover			
1844	9/17/11	Davidson	Yarbrough H.	Rebecca	
08/17/1838	5/27/20	Perquimans	Henry	Mary Beavers	
1849	4/29/09	Guilford			

D	S	G	RANK	LAST	GIVEN		CO	NR	UNIT
2	1	66	Pvt	Smith	Thomas M.	(M)	F	3	NC
5	1	317	Pvt	Smith	W. H.		F	5	Ga Vol Inf
1	1	Arl	Pvt	Smith	William L.		I	5	NC
5	1	349	Pvt	Smithwick	George W.		C		Ga Phillips' Leg
5	1	347	Pvt	Smithwick	John W.		C		Ga Phillips' Leg
2	1	57	Pvt	Sneed	Thomas		K	43	NC
7	3	172	Pvt	Snider	Henry J.		A	60	NC
3	2	55	Sgt	Snider	Thomas L.		C	25	NC
8	3	141	Pvt	Snipes	Benjamin		C	24	NC
7	3	195	Pvt	Snow	Richard		F	37	Va Batt Cav
4	1	N1	Col	Snyder	Peter			7	Ark Inf
6	1	523	Corp	Sorey	Dorsey W.		H	12	NC
7	1	402	Pvt	Sorrill	H. M.		A	5	SC Batt (Gile's)
7	1	376	Pvt	Southerland	Joseph B.		F	2	SC Cav
6	1	514	Pvt	Spainhour	Jacob Peter		D	53	NC
7	3	223	Pvt	Spaugh	George S.		K	21	NC
3	2	122	Capt	Spencer	Alexander Farrar		D	12	NC (2nd co)
8	3	27	Pvt	Spight	Jesse W.		B	24	NC
3	2	62	Pvt	Sprinkle	John		D	42	NC
2	1	62	Pvt	Stafford	Francis M.		G	16	NC
8	3	102	Pvt	Stafford	John H.		K	35	NC
7	1	369	Pvt	Staggers	John W.		C		SC Merriweather's Bn
4	2	200	Pvt	Stanford	Leonidas		C	51	NC
1	1	Arl	Pvt	Stansell	Winchester		C	43	NC
4	1	259	Pvt	Staples	Caleb R.		B	68	NC
7	1	368	Pvt	Stark	John		F	3	SC Batt Jr Res
6	1	468	Pvt	Steel	Robert C.		I	7	NC
4	1	300	Pvt	Steelman	George		H	63	NC (5 Cav)
3	1	163	—	* Stephens	J. R.		D	46	NC
1	1	Arl	Pvt	Stephens	Martin		D	7	NC
3	1	100	Pvt	Stephens	William L.	(M)	B	31	NC
7	3	202	Pvt	Stephenson	Alfred		C	5	NC
1	1	Arl	Corp	Stepps	George W.		C	20	NC
3	2	108	Pvt	Stevenson	Alexander		G	53	NC
1	1	Arl	Pvt	Stirewalt	Anderson G.		G	5	NC
4	1	286	Pvt	Stone	David W.		E	70	NC (1 Jr Res)
1	1	39	Pvt	Stone	Duncan E.		C	1	NC Batt H Art
6	1	526	Pvt	Strader	John Neubel		H	45	NC
8	3	109	Corp	Strayhorn	Baker W.		G	40	NC (3 Arty)
8	3	43	Pvt	Streeter	Elijah		B	31	NC
3	2	51	Pvt	Strickland	Haywood W.		B	20	NC
7	3	267	Pvt	Strickland	Isaac		C	3	NC Batt L Art
8	1	432	Pvt	Strickland	William M.		H	23	Ala
7	3	321	Pvt	Stubbins	Joseph Benjamin		G	44	NC

A Story Behind Every Stone

BIRTH	DEATH	COUNTY	FATHER	MOTHER	WIFE
1836	05/03/1865	Brunswick	Michael B.	Ann	
	03/25/1865				
1840	05/31/1864	Halifax			Sarah J. Carter
1844	08/13/1864	Cherokee	Tyro H.	Martha	
1842	08/10/1864	Cherokee	Tyro H.	Martha	
1844	05/26/1862	Anson			
12/10/1831	5/15/17	Lincoln	John	Racheal Coffee	
1844	05/23/1899	Haywood	Caleb	Sarah McGee	Mary Brendle
06/ /1838	7/31/15	Wake	David	Sealey Brown	Tempy Stell
10/27/1844	11/22/18	Surry	Isaac	Mickey Norman	
11/ /1829	04/19/1865		Theobald	Louisa Klein	Marietta A. Ayers
1841	07/11/1863	Nash			
	03/16/1865				
	02/10/1865	Pickens			
1841	07/25/1863	Stokes	John J.	Katherine	
01/07/1839	6/1/20	Forsyth	George	Elizabeth Sheets	
1828	3/18/05	Granville	Abraham B.	Martha Farrar	Sarah T. Paschall
1835	6/22/11	Onslow	Miles W.	Mary	
1820	7/11/00	Iredell			Sally
1838	09/01/1862	Rutherford		Sarah	
01/ /1848	3/12/14	McDowell			
	03/24/1865	Williamsburg			T.L.
08/ /1845	1/6/09	Duplin	Alexander	Martha W. Dickson	Elizabeth Hale
1841	07/19/1864	Wilson	William	Milley	
1832	06/12/1864	Camden	J.P.	Sarah	
	03/24/1865				
1834	08/27/1863	Iredell	Thomas	Nancy	
1837	12/26/1864	Davie	Charles		Jane
1831	05/24/1864				
1840	../../1865	Union	Christopher	Cathrine	
03/09/1834	2/9/19	Johnston	Soloman	Cressie Johnson	
1838	06/09/1864	Horry			
1827	6/17/04	Stokes			
1837	06/04/1864	Rowan	Daniel		
1846	09/26/1864	Moore	James D.	Judy Parrish	
1846	03/29/1865	Robeson	Hardy J.	Helen Ivey	
1844	07/20/1863	Rockingham		Sallie T.Ratliff	
07/12/1844	5/9/14	Orange	James	Rachael Cabe	
09/ /1832	12/26/11	Anson			
1844	06/16/1898	Cumberland			
1842	11/3/23	Johnston	Lewis	Leviel	
	03/30/1865				
05/12/1844	2/25/31	Alamance	Enoch	Nancy Crutchfield	

D	S	G	RANK	LAST	GIVEN	CO	NR	UNIT
6	1	549	Pvt	Sudderth	George Murray	I	26	NC
1	1	Arl	Pvt	Suitz	William M.	F	45	NC
7	3	240	Pvt	Summerour	John Calvin	I	26	NC
8	3	62	Pvt	Summers	William N.	K	13	NC
2	1	69	—	* Sumner	Joseph (CM)			NC
7	3	269	Pvt	Sutton	Martin V. B.	K	18	NC
3	2	38	Pvt	Sutton	William T.	H	9	NC (1 Cav)
3	1	130	Pvt	Swain	Benjamin F.	E	17	NC
3	2	91	Pvt	Swain	John G.	H	17	NC
7	1	374	Pvt	Swartz	Jasper M.	C	20	SC Inf
7	3	258	2ndSgt	Syme	John Cameron	C	47	NC
1	1	Arl	Pvt	Taber	Calvin C.	G	5	NC
7	3	231	Sgt	Tarkenton	Cornelius	B	3	NC Batt L Art
2	1	85	Pvt	Tarkenton	John (CM)	B	3	NC Batt L Art
1	2	30	Pvt	Tate	Robert W. E.	C	46	NC
8	3	143	Pvt	Tatum	Thaddeus C.	G	59	NC (4 Cav)
1	2	24	Pvt	Taylor	Benjamin F.	G	14	NC
7	3	265	Pvt	Taylor	Benjamin W.			Va Branch Art
4	2	201	Pvt	Taylor	Calvin	E	16	NC
4	1	238	Pvt	Taylor	William	A	17	NC
8	3	98	Pvt	Taylor	William H.	F		NC Mallett's Ba
7	3	207	Pvt	Teague	William R.	H	52	Ga Vol Inf
7	3	161	Pvt	Teal	James W.	I	43	NC
7	3	286	Pvt	Teasley	Willie W.	A	66	NC
1	2	SE2	Pvt	Terrell	James R.	B	59	NC (4 Cav)
6	1	492	Pvt	Terrell	William P.	H	45	NC
8	3	149	Sgt	Terry	Joseph E.		13	Va Batt Arty
6	1	516	Pvt	Tew	Ashley B.	E	20	NC
4	1	269	2nCorp	Tew	Jesse	A	71	NC (2 Jr Res)
4	2	169	Pvt	Therrell	James W.	F	35	NC
1	2	2	Pvt	Thomas	John W.	I	47	NC
3	2	39	AssQM	Thomas	Lewis L.		6	NC Sen Res(F8
3	2	60	Pvt	Thomas	Washington	B	63	NC (5 Cav)
4	1	287	Pvt	Thompson	Falcon	A	70	NC (1 Jr Res)
7	3	211	Corp	Thompson	James William	E	47	Va
6	1	484	Pvt	Thompson	Risden N.	I	52	NC
6	1	454	Sgt	Thompson	Thomas B.	G	52	NC
7	3	260	Pvt	Thompson	William Monroe	E	13	NC
7	1	399	—	* Threwpest	L. A.	K	1	SC
7	3	216	Pvt	Thrift	John W.	L	22	NC
8	1	431	Pvt	Tibbs	James K.	F	50	Ala
6	1	509	Sgt	Tilley	Robert P.	G	53	NC
8	3	95	2nd Lt	Tisdale	George F.	C	61	NC
3	2	42	Pvt	Topps	Richard S.	D	8	NC

A Story Behind Every Stone

BIRTH	DEATH	COUNTY	FATHER	MOTHER	WIFE
1843	07/01/1863	Caldwell	James	Jane Crider	
1844	08/21/1864	Rockingham	Jonathan	Susannah	
)4/07/1845	9/3/21	Caldwell	Joseph	Rachel Z. Turner	
1838	6/24/12	Rockingham	Andrew	Juliee	
)4/11/1841	2/28/24	Bladen	William T.	Mary Mulphodd	
1824	02/25/1896	Lenoir			
1837	08/25/1862	Martin	Ransom		
07/ /1843	1/6/03	Washington	Joshua	Frances	
	02/27/1865	Lexington	Adam	Susanna	
12/ /1843	12/30/22	Wake	J.W.	Mary Madden	
1842	04/16/1865	Buncombe			
1/09/1841	11/17/20	Washington	James	Nancy Speigh	
1838	03/28/1862	Tyrrell			
02/ /1831	06/21/1895	Warren			
1840	12/10/15	Currituck			
1839	10/07/1894	Rockingham	John P. Taylor	Elizabeth	
•9/10/1843	6/6/23	Durham	Benjamin	Martha Dormeright	
1832	2/28/09	Burke			
1840	04/22/1865	Martin			
02/ /1831	1/20/14	Onslow			
•4/17/1843	6/1/19	Fannin	Mangus	Elvira Ledford	
05/ /1836	10/12/16	Anson	William Luther	Sarah McKay	
•3/26/1836	11/23/25	Orange	Edward	Elnora Camington	
	01/01/1891	(Caswell)			
1836	07/07/1863	Rockingham	Soloman	Nancy	Frances E.
05/ /1835	3/18/16	Guilford			
1835	07/03/1863	Wayne	Daniel	Rebecca Dorman	Charity Outlaw
1847	11/29/1864	Sampson	Jesse	Winnie	
1836	7/7/07	Union			Nancy
1813	10/21/1891	Wake			Catherine
1818	04/23/1896	Davidson			Martha M.
1842	2/17/00	Carteret	Marcus C.	Elizabeth K.	
1/03/1847	11/20/1864	Warren			
0/15/1845	1/20/20	Northampton	W.D.	Mary R. Gray	
1845	09/25/1863	Stanly	D.K.	Eliza	
1833	08/10/1863	Lincoln	Thomas	Frances	
12/ /1840	1/16/23	Alamance			
	09/01/1863				
5/05/1846	3/20/20	Randolph	Isham	Mary Hindley	
1838	04/23/1865	Tuscaloosa			Mary J.
1844	07/04/1863	Stokes	David	Polly	
)4/ /1838	9/28/13	Craven	William	Sarah	
1827	05/08/1896	Warren			

A Story Behind Every Stone

D	S	G	RANK	LAST	GIVEN	CO	NR	UNIT
8	3	96	Pvt	Townsend	Ewing W.	B	29	NC
6	1	522	Sgt	Traynham	William B.	B	20	NC
3	2	97	Pvt	Treadwell	John R.	K	51	NC
7	3	305	Pvt	Trexler	Rufus T.	B	46	NC
1	1	2	Pvt	Trivett	John	B	42	NC
1	1	Arl	Pvt	Troxler	George S.	A	53	NC
6	1	459	1stSgt	Tucker	James G.	F	53	Va
7	3	169	Pvt	Turbyfill	WIlliam A.			SC Col Rob
5	2	S14	Lt Col	Turner	J. McLeod		7	NC
8	3	45	Pvt	Turner	John B.			Va Danville
6	1	438	Capt	Turner	John Calvin	D	23	Miss
3	2	110	3rd Lt	Turner	Julian S.	K	19	NC (2 Cav)
6	1	453	Pvt	* Turner	T. J.		2	NC
3	2	75	Pvt	Tuton	John	A	3	NC
1	1	5	Pvt	Underhill	John	C	1	NC Batt H
3	2	129	Pvt	Ungar	Lawrence	G	50	NC
3	2	78	.	unknown		.	.	.
3	1	106	.	unknown			46	NC
3	1	116	.	unknown		.	.	NC
3	1	117	.	unknown		.	.	NC
3	1	125	.	unknown			57	NC
3	1	138	.	unknown		.	.	NC
3	1	142	.	unknown		.	.	NC
3	1	144	.	unknown		.	.	NC
3	1	148	.	unknown		.	.	NC
3	1	150	.	unknown		.	.	NC
3	1	152	.	unknown		.	.	NC
3	1	155	.	unknown		.	.	NC
3	1	157	.	unknown		.	.	NC
3	1	158	.	unknown		.	.	NC
3	1	159	.	unknown		.	.	NC
3	1	166	.	unknown		.	.	NC
3	1	167	.	unknown		.	.	NC
3	1	169	.	unknown		.	.	NC
3	1	172	.	unknown		.	.	NC
3	1	175	.	unknown		.	.	NC
3	1	177	.	unknown		.	.	NC
3	1	178	.	unknown		.	.	NC
3	1	181	.	unknown		.	.	NC
3	1	188	.	unknown		.	.	NC
3	1	190	.	unknown		.	.	NC
3	1	197	.	unknown		.	.	NC
3	1	205	.	unknown		.	.	NC
3	1	218	.	unknown		.	.	NC

A Story Behind Every Stone

BIRTH	DEATH	COUNTY	FATHER	MOTHER	WIFE
11/ /1833	1/4/14	Buncombe			
1839	07/09/1863	Davidson	Jeffery P.	S.F.	
1834	3/12/03	Sampson	John	Charlotte Robinson	
05/ /1840	8/1/27	Rowan	John	Margaret	S.M.
	02/05/1865				
1824	05/05/1865	Guilford			
	08/12/1863				
1847	2/11/17	Bertie			
02/26/1841	09/24/1882				
08/ /1825	1/20/12	Iredell			
1832	03/30/1865	Hardeman	John	Winneford White	Sarah Elizabeth Warren
1833	9/9/04	Orange			
	08/01/1863				
05/ /1834	11/8/01	Greene			
1827	03/24/1865	Wayne			Susan
1824	9/5/05	Rutherford			

11/21/1862

D	S	G	RANK	LAST	GIVEN	CO	NR	UNIT
3	1	220	.	unknown		.	.	NC
3	1	222	.	unknown		.	.	NC
3	1	223	.	unknown		.	.	NC
3	1	225	.	unknown		.	.	NC
3	1	227	.	unknown		.	.	NC
4	1	249	.	unknown		.	.	NC
4	1	278	.	unknown		.	.	NC
4	1	280	.	unknown		.	.	NC
5	1	341	.	unknown		.	.	Ga
6	1	362	.	unknown		.	31	Miss
7	1	561	.	unknown		.	.	.
7	1	562	.	unknown		.	.	.
7	1	563	.	unknown		.	.	.
7	1	564	.	unknown		.	.	.
7	1	565	.	unknown		.	.	.
7	1	566	.	unknown		.	.	.
7	1	567	.	unknown		.	.	.
7	1	568	.	unknown		.	.	.
7	1	569	.	unknown		.	.	.
7	1	570	.	unknown		.	.	.
7	1	571	.	unknown		.	.	.
7	1	572	.	unknown		.	.	.
7	1	573	.	unknown		.	.	.
7	1	574	.	unknown		.	.	.
7	1	575	.	unknown		.	.	.
7	1	576	.	unknown		.	.	.
7	1	577	.	unknown		.	.	.
7	1	578	.	unknown		.	.	.
7	1	579	.	unknown		.	.	.
7	1	580	.	unknown		.	.	.
7	1	581	.	unknown		.	.	.
7	1	582	.	unknown		.	.	.
7	1	583	.	unknown		.	.	.
7	1	584	.	unknown		.	.	.
7	1	585	.	unknown		.	.	.
7	1	586	.	unknown		.	.	.
7	1	587	.	unknown		.	.	.
7	1	588	.	unknown		.	.	.
7	1	589	.	unknown		.	.	.
7	1	590	.	unknown		.	.	.
7	1	591	.	unknown		.	.	.
7	1	592	.	unknown		.	.	.
7	1	593	.	unknown		.	.	.
7	1	594	.	unknown		.	.	.

A Story Behind Every Stone

BIRTH	DEATH	COUNTY	FATHER	MOTHER	WIFE
	03/19/1865				

A Story Behind Every Stone

D	S	G	RANK	LAST	GIVEN	CO	NR	UNIT
7	1	595	.	unknown		.	.	.
7	1	596	.	unknown		.	.	.
7	1	597	.	unknown		.	.	.
7	1	598	.	unknown		.	.	.
7	1	599	.	unknown		.	.	.
7	1	600	.	unknown		.	.	.
7	1	601	.	unknown		.	.	.
7	1	602	.	unknown		.	.	.
7	1	603	.	unknown		.	.	.
7	1	604	.	unknown		.	.	.
7	1	605	.	unknown		.	.	.
7	1	606	.	unknown		.	.	.
7	1	607	.	unknown		.	.	.
7	1	608	.	unknown		.	.	.
7	1	609	.	unknown		.	.	.
7	1	610	.	unknown		.	.	.
7	1	611	.	unknown		.	.	.
7	1	612	.	unknown		.	.	.
7	1	613	.	unknown		.	.	.
7	1	614	.	unknown		.	.	.
7	1	615	.	unknown		.	.	.
7	1	616	.	unknown		.	.	.
7	1	617	.	unknown		.	.	.
7	1	618	.	unknown		.	.	.
8	1	619	.	unknown		.	.	.
8	1	620	.	unknown		.	.	.
8	1	621	.	unknown		.	.	.
8	1	622	.	unknown		.	.	.
8	1	623	.	unknown		.	.	.
8	1	624	.	unknown		.	.	.
8	1	625	.	unknown		.	.	.
8	1	626	.	unknown		.	.	.
8	1	627	.	unknown		.	.	.
8	1	628	.	unknown		.	.	.
8	1	629	.	unknown		.	.	.
8	1	630	.	unknown		.	.	.
8	1	631	.	unknown		.	.	.
8	1	632	.	unknown		.	.	.
8	1	633	.	unknown		.	.	.
8	1	634	.	unknown		.	.	.
8	1	635	.	unknown		.	.	.
8	1	636	.	unknown		.	.	.
8	1	637	.	unknown		.	.	.
8	1	638	.	unknown		.	.	.

A Story Behind Every Stone

BIRTH	DEATH	COUNTY	FATHER	MOTHER	WIFE

A Story Behind Every Stone

D	S	G	RANK	LAST	GIVEN	CO	NR	UNIT
8	1	639	.	unknown		.	.	.
8	1	640	.	unknown		.	.	.
8	1	641	.	unknown		.	.	.
8	1	642	.	unknown		.	.	.
8	1	643	.	unknown		.	.	.
8	1	644	.	unknown		.	.	.
8	1	645	.	unknown		.	.	.
8	1	646	.	unknown		.	.	.
8	1	647	.	unknown		.	.	.
8	1	648	.	unknown		.	.	.
8	1	649	.	unknown		.	.	.
8	1	650	.	unknown		.	..	.
8	1	651	.	unknown		.	.	.
8	1	652	.	unknown		.	.	.
8	1	653	.	unknown		.	.	.
8	1	654	.	unknown		.	.	.
8	1	655	.	unknown		.	.	.
8	1	656	.	unknown		.	.	.
8	1	657	.	unknown		.	.	.
8	1	658	.	unknown		.	.	.
8	1	659	.	unknown		.	.	.
8	1	660	.	unknown		.	.	.
8	1	661	.	unknown		.	.	.
8	1	662	.	unknown		.	.	.
8	1	663	.	unknown		.	.	.
8	1	664	.	unknown		.	.	.
8	1	665	.	unknown		.	.	.
8	1	666	.	unknown		.	.	.
1	1	Arl	.	unknown		H	48	NC
4	1	N5	.	unknown		.	..	
8	1	N7	.	unknown		.	.	.
5	1	S17	.	unknown	Cold Harbor		.	NC
3	2	142	Pvt	Upchurch	Green Berry	D	33	NC
3	1	111	—	*Vance	J. M.			NC
8	3	57	1stSgt	Vaughn	Azariah A.	D	45	NC
8	3	72	Pvt	Vaughn	Mitchell Benjamin	E	45	NC
6	1	507	Pvt	Vick	William H.	D	32	NC
3	2	64	Pvt	Vogler	George E.	I	2	NC
3	2	89	Pvt	Wade	Henry R.	D	59	NC (4 Cav)
4	1	308	Pvt	Wade	John Louis	I	51	NC
6	1	499	Pvt	Wade	Littleton R.	E	32	NC
6	1	451	Pvt	Waesner	Solomon Ephraim	E	28	NC
2	1	91	Pvt	Waldrop	William W. (CC)	G	35	NC
6	1	457	Pvt	Walker	Benjamin Frederick	I	30	NC

A Story Behind Every Stone

BIRTH	DEATH	COUNTY	FATHER	MOTHER	WIFE
09/ /1824	9/8/06	Wake	Hubard	Esther	Mariah
07/27/1836	5/2/12	Rockingham			Martha Jane Humphreys
1830	10/9/12	Rockingham	Franklin	Mary J.	Lucy
1834	07/01/1863	Northampton		Matilda	
12/21/1837	9/4/00	Craven	John M.	Marah	
1832	9/22/02	Northampton			
1845	03/30/1865	Cumberland	Levi C.	Christian	
1846	07/07/1863	Catawba	Richard	Harriette	
1835	08/18/1863	Montgomery	David	A.M.	
1843	11/19/1861	Henderson			
1832	08/12/1863	Nash		Susan	

A Story Behind Every Stone

D	S	G	RANK	LAST	GIVEN	CO	NR	UNIT
8	3	25	Pvt	Walker	Carey Willams	K	55	NC
1	1	34	Pvt	Walker	David	C	3	NC Batt Sen ▶
3	2	47	Pvt	Walker	David A.	H	6	NC
6	1	524	—	* Walker	E. W.			NC
4	2	153	2nd Lt	Walker	Hardy F.	G	45	NC
6	1	540	Corp	Walker	Marshall H.	H	6	NC
3	2	76	Pvt	Walker	William A.	K	13	NC
4	2	208	Pvt	Wall	John W.	E	47	NC
6	1	527	—	* Wallace	J. A.			NC
4	2	213	Pvt	Wallace	John M.	E	59	NC (4 Cav)
7	3	210	Pvt	Waller	Louis A.	I	66	NC
3	1	162	Pvt	Walls	William (WF)	H	70	NC (1 Jr Res)
8	1	425	Lt	Walsh			11	Texas Cav
4	1	293	Pvt	Warlick	J. Franklin	D	2	NC Jr Res
3	1	143	Pvt	Warren	J. H.	C		NC Camp Gu
7	3	287	Pvt	Warren	James M.	I	25	NC
4	1	283	Pvt	Waters	James Oliver	F	18	NC
8	1	434	Pvt	Waters	John W.	H	18	Ala
7	3	191	2nd Lt	Watkins	Archer W.	H	45	NC
3	1	217	Pvt	Watkins	Arnel	K	60	NC
6	1	501	Sgt	Watkins	Charles A.	H	45	NC
4	1	315	—	* Watkins	Peter			NC
3	1	186	Pvt	Watkins	Simeon O.	G	56	NC
8	3	125	Pvt	Watson	Edward David	I	21	NC
7	3	185	Pvt	Watson	Franklin L.	I	67	NC
7	1	372	Pvt	Watson	J. M.	H	4	SC Cav
3	1	154	Pvt	Watters	David W.	D	15	NC
7	3	232	Pvt	Watts	Jessie D.	I	7	NC
7	1	397	Pvt	Watts	John B.	A		SC Hampton's Legior
8	3	49	Pvt	Weathersbee	Henry Walter	G	18	Miss
8	3	80	Pvt	Webster	John F.	A	21	NC
6	1	544	Pvt	Weeden	Robert A.	K	47	NC
5	1	339	Pvt	Weeks	David	A	20	Ga Batt Cav
3	2	120	Pvt	Wells	Anderson	G	26	NC
2	1	63	—	* Werrell	B. B.			NC
3	1	213	Pvt	West	Anderson	E	44	NC
3	1	101	Pvt	West	James	A	46	NC
4	2	187	Pvt	West	William C.	B	10	NC (1 Art)
1	1	Arl	Pvt	Westbrook	Moses F.	H	20	NC
7	3	294	Pvt	Wheeler	Charles H.			NC
2	1	49	5thSgt	Wheeling	Carson E.C.	K	53	NC
1	1	16	Pvt	Whisenhunt	William	G	72	NC (3 Jr Res)
7	3	281	Pvt	Whitaker	James Reid	K	10	NC (1 Art)
1	1	Arl	Pvt	Whitaker	Martin F.	H	21	NC

A Story Behind Every Stone

BIRTH	DEATH	COUNTY	FATHER	MOTHER	WIFE
11/ /1841	5/11/11	Person	Solomon	Nancy	
10/ /1815	03/19/1865	Franklin			
1842	02/28/1897	Caswell	Abner	Margaret A.	
	../../1863				
1839	1/9/07	Rockingham			
1841	07/01/1863	Caswell	James	Mildred	
02/ /1824	12/26/01	Rockingham			Laura A.
02/ /1847	7/2/09	Wake			
	07/03/1863				
1837	8/31/09	Cabarrus			
04/22/1840	11/29/19	Lenoir	Willis	Eliza Bowman	
1847	03/30/1865				
	04/13/1865				
12/4/1846	08/11/1864	Cleveland	John	Jane Boggs	
	07/02/1863				
05/ /1840	1/16/26	Buncombe	John	Betsy	Rosa
1844	../../1865	Rutherford	Thomas	Olly	
1837	04/03/1865	Pike			
08/11/1844	8/26/18	Rockingham	John G.	Nancy Royall	
	01/10/1864	Burke			
1844	07/23/1863	Rockingham	Frances	Martha R.	
1837	12/18/1863	Henderson			
1843	1/24/15	Surry	James	Lucinda	
07/20/1837	5/24/18	Craven	Nathan	Barbara Privett	
	03/16/1864	Lexington			
1838	09/23/1862	Rutherford	James	Sarah	
04/20/1843	12/21/20	Iredell	Enoch	Margaretta Alley	
	07/07/1864				
1829	2/18/12	Madison			
01/ /1837	2/22/13	Stokes	J.H.	Bettie	
1842	07/23/1863	Alamance	H.	Sarah	
	08/04/1864		Michael	Judith Ann Gennett	Frances Drowdy
05/ /1825	2/17/05	Chatham			Sarah
1841	01/27/1863	Randolph			
1836	05/12/1862	Robeson			
1832	4/5/08	Craven	Riley	Mary	
1840	06/15/1865	Sampson			
08/10/1845	7/21/26	Johnston			
1825	06/06/1862	Wilkes			Martha
1847	03/09/1865	Burke	Harvey	Sarah A.	
03/ /1842	7/27/25	Beaufort			
1845	04/06/1865	Surry	Silas	Elizabeth Cooper	

D	S	G	RANK	LAST	GIVEN	CO	NR	UNIT
6	1	455	Pvt	White	Henry	C	55	NC
4	1	264	Corp	White	James K.	B	24	NC
7	3	243	Pvt	White	Kenneth Raynor	A	13	NC Batt L Art
4	1	253	Pvt	White	Lanor	H	11	NC
7	1	406	Pvt	White	William H.	I	16	SC Inf
4	2	204	Pvt	Whitehead	Asbury	D	43	NC
4	1	266	Pvt	Whitehurst	Henry	B	68	NC
4	2	209	Capt	Whitehurst	James J.	K	10	NC (1 Art)
2	2	SE3	Capt	Whiting	George Mordecai	C	47	NC
3	1	174	—	*Whiting	H.			NC
3	2	83	Pvt	Whitley	James Thaddeus	K	66	NC
7	3	250	Pvt	Wiggins	John A.	B	25	NC
7	3	308	Pvt	Wilborn	Thomas Jefferson	C	70	NC (1 Jr Res)
7	3	315	Pvt	Wilkins	John W.	E	24	NC
5	3	S2	Pvt	Wilkins	Roscoe W.	I	10	NC (1 Arty)
3	1	103	2nd Lt	Wilkinson	John W.	I	71	NC (2 Jr Res)
6	1	537	Pvt	Willcox	Harmon Husband	H	26	NC
7	3	317	Pvt	Williams	James A.	H	63	NC (5 Cav)
6	1	547	Pvt	Williams	James M.	I	6	NC
6	1	550	2nd Lt	Williams	James W.	G	11	NC
3	2	58	AsSurg	Williams	John M., Dr.		26	Texas Cav F &
7	3	174	Pvt	Williams	John Wesley	H	47	NC
4	2	183	Pvt	Williams	Tyree G.	I	33	NC
4	2	181	Pvt	Williams	Vinson W.	A	10	NC (1 Art)
6	1	534	Sgt	Williams	William A.	I	45	NC
8	3	35	Pvt	Williamson	James B.	B	24	NC
8	1	430	2ndLt	Williamson	William T.	C	1	Ala
6	1	449	Pvt	Williford	Thomas	G	2	NC
4	2	160	Pvt	Willis	Joseph F.	C	1	Navy Fla Batt
7	3	256	Pvt	Willis	William M.	H	10	NC (1 Art)
6	1	539	—	*Willis			6	NC
7	3	291	Pvt	Wilson	Chadmus Andrew	H	32	NC (2nd co)
3	1	210	Pvt	Wilson	Hubbard L.	L	21	NC
1	2	34	Pvt	Wilson	James Joseph	G	47	NC
3	2	139	Pvt	Wilson	John Tyler Monroe	H	50	NC
8	3	67	Pvt	Wilson	Mathias		30	NC
6	1	365	Pvt	Wilson	Neil A.	A	33	Miss
6	1	535	Capt	Wilson	William	B	26	NC
1	1	31	Pvt	Winders	W. Horace	D	63	NC (5 Cav)
3	1	153	Pvt	Winn	Benjamin F.	B	24	Ga Vol Inf
3	1	232	—	*Winston	William			NC
7	3	344	Pvt	Wise	Andrew J.	H	29	NC
7	3	327	Pvt	Witherington	James W.	C	70	NC (1 Jr Res)
3	1	216	Pvt	Womack	Jefferson	D	61	NC

A Story Behind Every Stone

BIRTH	DEATH	COUNTY	FATHER	MOTHER	WIFE
1837	08/08/1863	Cleveland	Isham	Junetta	Martha
1836	05/25/1864	Onslow			
04/05/1840	11/29/21	Perquimans	Abrabam	Mary E. Scott	
	07/ /1864				
1830	04/02/1865	Laurens			M.
1844	5/20/09	Halifax	Lawrence Hale	Emeliza White	Addie C. Howenton
1840	05/21/1864	Camden	Enoch	Nancy	
09/ /1837	7/23/09	Edgecombe			
1842	02/01/1870	Wake	S.W.	Hannah M.	
1842	6/8/02	Wilson	E. Gray	Elizabeth	
05/ /1843	5/8/22	Jackson			
09/14/1844	3/5/28	Davidson	Evans	Cloie Veach	
04/10/1842	3/18/29	Johnston	Oppie	Nancy King	
11/27/1845	5/16/37	Halifax	B.R.	Jane W. Hamill	
1847	03/25/1865	Beaufort	Robert J.	Mary	
2/25/45	07/02/1863	Moore	George	Margaret Martin	
11/18/1845	1/6/30	Davie	Martin	Charity Howard	
1842	07/02/1863	Chatham	Marmaduke	Penninah	
01/29/1839	07/01/1863	Orange			
1832	6/24/00	Davie			
06/12/1845	8/12/17	Wake	Benjamine	Beneline Wood	
1830	2/4/08	Forsyth			
05/11/1835	1/4/08	Wake	Joseph	Lotty	
1839	07/06/1863	Person	William	Mary	
1834	11/16/11	Onslow	Bryan	Polly	Susan A. Aman
1837		Lowndes	Arthur Fort	Martha	
1844	08/05/1863	Jones	Mike	Olivia	
09/ /1835	5/3/07	Bladen			
02/28/1842	12/3/22	Carteret	John	Josephine Golden	
	../../1863				
04/11/1839	2/28/26	Edgecombe	Acy	Emily Bullock	
1825	04/02/1864	Rockingham	Elijah	Nancy Ann Paschal	Frances Williams
06/14/1833	06/28/1894	Wake			Eliza Elizabeth
1844	8/21/06	Harnett	Anderson	Nancy	
04/ /1826	8/10/12	Randolph			Margaret
1846	03/22/1865	Leake	C.G.	Margaret Cone	
1842	07/01/1863	Union	Hugh	Sarah	
1837	03/07/1865	Duplin	Henry	Dorothy	Ann J.
02/24/1841	09/26/1862	Elbert	Gustavus Adolphus		Nancy Burden
1844	6/21/38	Buncombe	William	Margaret	
02/16/1847	8/31/32	Forsyth			
1839	01/29/1863	Chatham	James	Pity	

D	S	G	RANK	LAST	GIVEN	CO	NR	UNIT
3	1	200	Pvt	Woodard	Doctor Devroe	D	66	NC
8	3	59	Pvt	Woodard	Thomas	H	7	Conf Cav
4	2	N3	Pvt	Woodliff	Thomas D.	E	15	NC
5	1	331	Pvt	Woods	William	A	29	Ga Vol Inf
1	1	26	Pvt	Woodward	Henry	K	70	NC (1 Jr Res
1	1	42	2nCorp	Wooten	Allen W.	I	66	NC
6	1	508	Pvt	Workman	George W.	I	32	NC
8	3	3	Pvt	Worsham	John D.	C	13	NC
6	1	518	Pvt	Yancey	Simeon Peter	D	12	NC
8	3	19	Pvt	Yeargan	Daniel	M	22	NC
3	2	73	1st Lt	Young	Samuel A.	A	10	NC Batt H
8	3	134	Pvt	Young	Thomas L.	I	25	NC

A Story Behind Every Stone

BIRTH	DEATH	COUNTY	FATHER	MOTHER	WIFE
1826	09/08/1863	Johnston	Joseph	Patience Daughtry	Martha Massey
06/ /1830	5/23/12	Wilson			Sallie
1824	12/30/1895	Granville			Sarah
1847	04/23/1865	Screven		Templeton	
01/25/1847	09/25/1864	Northampton			
1846	03/28/1865	Lenoir	Allen W.	Tabitha	
1840	07/01/1863	Orange	Berry	Frances	
1840	12/13/09	Caswell			
1835	07/26/1863	Granville	Richard E.	Harriet P.	
1832	11/14/10	Randolph	Isaac	Milisant	
1837	9/28/01	Wake	Thomas	Rebecca Cutts	Julia Powell
10/ /1832	5/5/15	Buncombe			Martha

Oakwood Veterans By North Carolina Counties

NC County	No.
Alamance	19
Alexander	5
Alleghany	1
Anson	15
Ashe	5
Beaufort	11
Bertie	8
Bladen	10
Brunswick	3
Buncombe	13
Burke	10
Cabarrus	9
Caldwell	5
Camden	2
Carteret	3
Caswell	15
Catawba	11
Chatham	21
Chowan	2
Cleveland	12
Columbus	5
Craven	9
Cumberland	17
Currituck	6
Dare	1
Davidson	21
Davie	6
Duplin	12
Durham	1
Edgecombe	17

NC County	No.
Forsyth	8
Franklin	16
Gaston	5
Gates	6
Granville	30
Greene	9
Guilford	19
Halifax	23
Harnett	9
Haywood	7
Henderson	9
Hertford	6
Horry	1
Hyde	1
Iredell	14
Jackson	2
Johnston	16
Jones	3
Lenoir	16
Lincoln	14
Macon	1
Madison	5
Martin	16
McDowell	9
Meckenburg	10
Montgomery	4
Moore	15
Nash	13
New Hanover	11
Northampton	8

A Story Behind Every Stone

NC County	No.	NC County	No.
Onslow	9	Stokes	12
Orange	25	Surry	13
Pamlico	2	Swain	1
Pasquotank	5	Tyrrell	4
Pender	2	Union	21
Perquimans	3	Vance	1
Person	10	Wake	57
Pitt	16	Warren	17
Randolph	17	Washington	5
Richmond	4	Watauga	1
Robeson	15	Wayne	9
Rockingham	38	Wilkes	11
Rowan	10	Wilson	14
Rutherford	14	Yadkin	5
Sampson	14	Yancey	4
Scotland	1	**Total**	**953**
Stanly	12		

Oakwood Veterans By Rank and States

Rank	No.				
Corp, 1st	2	Sergeant	40	NC Unit	No.
Lt, 1st	7	Sgt Major	1	1 NC	11
Lt, 2nd	23	Surgeon	2	2 NC	11
Lt	4	Unknown	226	3 NC	11
Lt, 2nd Jr	1	**Total**	**1,386**	4 NC	9
Sgt, 1st	10			5 NC	18
Corp, 2nd	8	**State/Dept**	**No.**	6 NC	24
Sgt, 2nd	2	Unknown	125	7 NC	11
Lt, 3rd	5	Conf Cav	2	8 NC	13
Sgt, 3rd	2	Conf Eng	1	9 NC	14
Sgt, 4th	2	Med Dept	1	10 NC	27
Sgt, 5th	4	Ord Dept	1	11 NC	11
Adjutant	1	Pettigrew's	1	12 NC	14
Assit QM	1	Signal Corps	1	13 NC	16
Assit Surg	1	Alabama	14	14 NC	17
Captain	22	Arkansas	2	15 NC	10
Chaplain	1	Florida	3	16 NC	9
Colonel	3	Georgia	49	17 NC	25
Conscript	5	Louisiana	2	18 NC	10
Corpral	23	Mississippi	14	19 NC	15
Ensign	1	Missouri	2	20 NC	15
Gunner	1	Navy	8	21 NC	16
Landsman	2	NC	1071	22 NC	15
Lt Colonel	2	NY	1	23 NC	13
Major	1	SC	59	24 NC	12
Musician	9	Tennessee	4	25 NC	14
Private	972	Texas	3	26 NC	19
Quartermaster	1	Minnesota	1	27 NC	15
Seaman	1	Virginia	25	28 NC	15
		Total	**1,390**	29 NC	14

30 NC............13	62 NC...............3	16 Batt Cav.......5
31 NC............15	63 NC...............9	2 Batt.................8
32 NC............20	64 NC...............0	2 Batt Loc Def..1
33 NC............4	65 NC...............1	26 Batt.............1
34 NC............3	66 NC...............8	3 Batt L Arty.....9
35 NC............15	67 NC............12	3 Batt Sen Res...1
36 NC............8	68 NC............12	4 Batt Jr Res......2
37 NC............7	69 NC...............2	6 Sen Res 2
38 NC............5	70 NC............15	7 Sen Res 1
39 NC............0	71 NC............20	8 Batt.................1
40 NC............12	72 NC...............9	8 Batt Part Ran.1
41 NC............13	1 Conf Eng 1	8 Senior Res......1
42 NC............11	1 NC Eng 1	Camp Guard 1
43 NC............29	7 Conf...............2	Conscript 3
44 NC............19	Conscript Dept.1	Freeman's Batt...1
45 NC............34	Coyette's Batt....1	Home Guard.....4
46 NC............12	Fay Ars&Arm....1	Mallett's Batt.....5
47 NC............36	Jr Res 1	McDugald's 3
48 NC............12	Med Dept 1	McRae's Batt.....1
49 NC............9	NC Part Rang...1	Navy 8
50 NC............17	Ord Dept 1	Thomas' Legion 1
51 NC............14	Pettigrew's 1	
52 NC............17	Signal Corp.......1	
53 NC............23	Unknown........69	
54 NC............5	1 NC (6 Mo).....5	
55 NC............7	1 Batt H Arty....4	
56 NC............12	10 Batt H Arty..3	
57 NC............6	12 Batt Cav.......1	
58 NC............1	13 Batt L Arty...9	
59 NC............12	13 Battery.........1	
60 NC............4	14 Batt Cav.......1	
61 NC............7	15 Batt Cav.......2	

Occupations of Oakwood Veterans

APOTHECARY
Bingham, George Miller

BANK KEEPER
DeWitt, William L.

BAR KEEPER
Butt, Thaddeus W.

BLACKSMITH
Jenkins, William M.
Love, Robert
Spight, Jesse W.
Wells, Anderson

BOATSMAN
Hand, Owen
Ethridge, Amos R., Jr.

BOILERMAKER
Mahoney, James R.

BOOKKEEPER
Goodloe, Lewis D.

BRICK MAKER
Claytor, Samuel Baker

BUGLER
Gates, Dudley H.

BUTCHER
Gooch, William Lee

CABINETMAKER
Parrish, Uriah R.

CAMP GUARD
Hornback, Eli
Ruffin, Gray
Partin, Alexander

CARPENTER
Britt, Richard Thomas
Cochran, James W.
Cordon, William W.
Goodwin, George L.
Hackney, Thomas L.
Hagler, Darling M.
Holden, Sylvanus
Marshall, George William
Jarrett, Benjamin D.

CLERK
Hancock, John R.
Hoyt, James H.
Jones, Berry J.

COACH MAKER
Carson, James M.
Causey, Robertson C.
Joyner, James
Marshall, John W.
Pittman, James A.
Holland, William

COACH PAINTER
Johnston, John H.
Johnson, John W. H.

COOPER
Adams, William
Ballington, James N.
Brown, Owen M.
Henderson, Walter S.
Smith, Basil T.

COURIER
Brooks, John T.

DAY LABORER
Barnes, Jethro

DISPATCHER
FOR GENERAL LEE
Miller, Henry

DITCHER
Jones, Allen

DRUGGIST
Whiting, George Mordecai

DRUMMER
Ransdell, George W.

ENGINEER
Burgess, Hardy B.

FARMER
Abernathy, Marion C.
Adams, James A.
Adams, John F.
Alderman, Henry S.
Alexander, James W.
Alley, Andrew Leven
Almond, Calvin
Almond, William J.
Andrew, Samuels S. W.
Ard, James, Jr.
Austin, James G.
Ayers, Joshua Franklin
Baird, Thomas A.
Barker, Edward
Batchelor, William B.
(WF)
Baxter, Wallace B.
Beard, James F.
Beaver, George L.
Bennett, Joseph E.
Biggerstaff, Alfred Webb
Black, Samuel A.
Blackley, William J.
Blow, Richard
Boggan, William W.

A Story Behind Every Stone

Brackens, Adam
Brassell, Titus F.
Bray, William A.
Bridgers, Clements
Brigman, Anannias
Brinson, David H.
Britt, Edward
Brittain, Isaac James
Brooks, James
Brooks, Larkin B.
Brown, John
Brownlee, John H.
Bryant, Joseph John
Bryant, Stephen N.
Bunn, George W.
Butler, John S.
Byrd, Needham T.
Byrd, Thomas
Cain, Struly Howard
Capps, John
Carroll, Lewis
Carter, John   (M)
Carver, R. Elzey
Casper, Justin
Champion, Charles William
Chandler, James M.
Chapman, Richard A.
Chappell, Franklin T.
Cline, Gibson C.
Clopton, Thomas H.
Coe, William W.
Collins, James M.
Collins, John S.
Combs, Nelson
Cone, Thomas Jackson
Cox, Cornelius G.
Crabtree, Abram C.
Cranford, Wilburn M.
Crosswell, David O.
(M)
Cunningham, Jesse
Currie, John H.
Cuthrell, Samuel
Daniel, Benjamin F.

Danieley, Henry
Davis, Archibald J.
Davis, Logan C.
Dawson, Francis
Dees, Clement Allen
Dees, Newitt
Delamar, William Bryan
Dillard, Jacob
Dobson, John O.
Doggett, James G.
Doles, William F.
Dowden, Ezekiel
Dowdy, Caleb George
Dowell, Franklin
Duncan, Abraham D.
Duncan, Gordon Cawthorne
Edmonson, Andrew McDonnel
Ellis, Enoch Franklin
Emory, Ephraim
Eure, Alfred L.
Eure, Lafayette L.
Faggart, Paul A.
Falkner, William Martin
Fallin, Redmond T.
Ferrell, Thomas Jefferson
Fletcher, Matthew
Forrest, Samuel P.
Fowler, James W.
Fox, Cain
Freeman, William James
Gaddy, Stephen T.
Geringer, John H.
Gilbert, William
Gracie, John G.
Grant, James   (CM)
Gray, Timothy Iredell
Green, Drury A.
Green, James M.
Griffin, Claudius P.
Guy, Lewis H.
Hadley, William Blount
Hagler, Hiram
Hall, Harrison

Hampton, Wiley P.
Harden, George L.
Hardin, Zachariah C.
Harman, Henry Holmes
Harper, Allen
Harrell, John A.
Harris, William D.
Harrison, Walter N.
Hartgrave, Joseph F.
Hatch, James R.
Heard, John
Heavlin, Robert A.
Hedrick, William F.
Hefner, Sylvanus
Helms, Joshua
Henry, William L.
Herrington, John Kinder
Hill, Jonathan
Hoots, William
Hopkins, Barney H.
Hopkins, David Allen
Horton, James Wiley
Hubbard, George Dallas
Hudgins, R. B.
Hudson, Junius   (CC)
Humphrey, James Lee
Hunsucker, Daniel
Hyde, William Harvey
Ingram, John
Jackson, Shadrack
Jackson, Thomas
Jenkins, Ammon
Jenkins, Docton
(CC)
Jenkins, Robert M.
Jolly, Wesley
Jones, Alvis C.
Jones, ChristopherColumbus
Jones, McGilbert
Keith, Anderson Christopher
Keith, Thomas Jefferson
Kelly, William W.
King, Benjamin Franklin

King, Nathaniel E.
King, W. G.
Kirby, William C.
Luther, Franklin
McElhannon, George W.
McLean, Joseph M.
Morgan, Permenter B.
Morrison, Elam F.
Parker, Stephen R.
Richardson, William W.
Robinson, Joseph B.
Saunders, Robert J.
Short, James E.
Stafford, John H.
Taylor, Benjamin F.
Thompson, Risden N.
Thompson, Thomas B.
Tilley, Robert P.
Treadwell, John R.
Waldrop, William W.
(CC)
Watkins, Simeon O.
Wheeling, Carson E.C.
White, Henry

FARMHAND
Coppage, William F.

FARM LABOR
Cates, Ephraim
Alley, Isaiah D.
Beddingfield, Addison R.
Bryant, William T.
Claytor, Patrick Henry
Clippard, John A.
Cone, Neverson
Epps, William D.
Fleming, Thomas B.
(M)
Gay, Gilbert G.
Gunnell, James G.
Hazard, Samuel
Holloway, Nathaniel
Woodard

James, John W.
Jordan, Andrew J.
Kelly, John
Kennedy, John Thomas
Therrell, James W.

FIFER IN SOLDIERS HOME
Johnson, Wiley T.

FISHERMAN
Clagon, Benjamin W.

HARNESS MAKER
Kingsmore, Richard S.
Gurney, Ford

HOTELKEEPER
Thomas, Lewis L.

HOUSE CARPENTER
Fish, William Henry

INNKEEPER
Price, Thomas A.

IRON MASTER
Adkins, William H.

LABORER
Hager, Sidney H.
Ashley, Allen   (CC)
Aydolett, Francis Marion
Brown, William R.
Dearman, William F.
Farrington, Loton W.
Fields, Doctor G.
Godfrey, Richmond
Harris, Samuel
Holloway, Martin
(CC)
King, Wiley D.
Perry, James R.

LAWYER
Arthur, Thomas S.
Whiting, George Mordecai

LIBRARIAN ATTENDANT
Ballew, James S.

LUMBER INSPECTOR
Gray, Timothy Iredell

MACHINIST
Nowell, Ransom Green
Smith, Thomas M.

MARINER
Crain, Jesse
Howland, Samuel L.

MASON
Bigham, John Robert
Spencer, Alexander Farrar

MASTER TANNER
Aderholt, Jacob E.

MECHANIC
Aldridge, Bennett Franklin
Ballentine, Jonathan L.
Hartsell, Jonah A.
Hopkins, James Franklin
Jernigan, William H.
Parker, William H.
Parker, William Howel
Ungar, Lawrence
Walker, David
Jarrett, Benjamin D.
Gurney, Ford

MERCHANT
Broom, Solomon S.
Fowler, Joseph S.
House, James
DeWitt, William L.

124

Hopkins, Barney H.
MERCHANT CLERK
Ferguson, George P.
Morrison, Elam F.

MILL HAND
Johns, John A.

MILLER
Pace, Edward
Sauls, Rufus A.
Taylor, Calvin
Harrison, William J.

NIGHTWATCHMAN
AT STATE CAPITOL
Barkley, Britton L.

OVERSEER
Arledge, James L.
Cobler, John H.
Estes, Richard B.
Goodwin, Ebenezer J.
Hays, John
Vick, William H.

PAINTER
Atkins, William H.
Hoyle, James R.
Hundley, John A.

PRINTER
Gilbert, Martin Van Buren
Jones, Josiah
Lee, Thomas G.
McLendon, John C.

PHYSICIAN
Duggan, William A., Dr.
Hines, James M.
Ramseur, David P.
Staggers, John W.

QUARTERMASTER
Shaw, William W.

SADDLER
Hasten, William
Gurney, Ford

SALESMAN
Hawkins, Dallas

SAWMILL WORKER
Page, Marion Dempsey

SCHOOL TEACHER
Bailey, Edward L.
Brame, Tignal H.
Gardner, James Lafayette
Harrison, William J.
Hasten, William
Henkle, William O.
Hoey, John E.
Waesner, Solomon
Ephraim
Walker, Hardy F.

SEA CAPTAIN
Melson, John A.

SHOEMAKER
Boon, Jacob C.
Franklin, John H.
Hamilton, Wesley G.
Mangum, Peter J.
Pilkinton, Joseph A.

STAGE DRIVER
Smith, John W.

STEVEDOR IN
SAVANNAH
Patrick, Dennis M.

STONEMASON
Leighton, John Henry
Lyman, William

STORE CLERK
Banks, Harrison

STUDENT IN
COLLEGE
Wilson, William

STUDENT OF
DIVINITY
Arent, William R.

TAILOR
Coleman, Daniel M.
Dancy, William
Miller, Joseph A.
Smith, Balthrop

TOBACCO TRADER
Dement, Alfonzo J.

TURPENTINE
LABORER
Prince, John

WAGGONER
McKinney, Moses J.

WAITER IN
PETERBURG
RESTAURANT
Parsons, William Holt

WHEELWRIGHT
Perdue, William

A Story Behind Every Stone

LaVergne, TN USA
02 November 2010
202938LV00004B/1/P